Introduction

I0040795

Communication is the key to life. From corporate presentations and job interviews to personal conflicts and interpersonal communications, our success in life - and in any given moment - often relies on our ability to successfully transmit an important message to others. Anyone who has ever engaged in a dispute with his or her spouse, boss, or child can attest to the fact that effectively communicating a message to even one person is a challenge (particularly when that person is not motivated to see things from your perspective). Individuals who rely on their ability to communicate for their livelihood, such as corporate presenters or sales people, face an even more daunting task: effectively communicating a message to each participant in the audience, regardless of whether that participant is receptive to the message or not.

In response to these challenges, Carolina Rodriguez, a Six Sigma Master Black Belt Specialist, began developing an improved communication model for communicators, leaders, and managers. Her work resulted in the Skill and Will Quadrant, an innovative approach to personal and professional communication. Modeled from Ken Blanchard's Blanchard Situational Leadership Model, the Quadrant was designed to help communicators learn how to best connect with each of their listeners, whether in a one-on-one dialogue or in a presentation to a large audience.

Rodriguez identifies and explains the effect of a listener's level of motivation (will) and training (skill) on his *ability* and *willingness* to understand a message. In the simple but ever-changing relationship between skill and will, an individual's will is controlled by his level of skill. Inversely, a person's level of skill is affected by his level of will. In terms of communication, some listeners do not have the skill to comprehend a message, while others lack the desire or motivation to try (will). Identifying and placing participants in the Quadrant – and understanding why each participant falls into that specific category – enables communicators to effectively prepare the participant to hear and comprehend the message.

Identifying and understanding quadrant placement also helps leaders shift participants from their current level of skill and will to a higher placement in the quadrant. For instance, a low will, high skill participant can be moved to a high will, high skill placement if the communicator is able to assess and appropriately motivate that individual to hear the message. Rodriguez offers helpful suggestions for leaders and communicators on how to assess their recipient's level of skill and will and tailor their message to appeal to the recipient.

By learning how to place individuals in the appropriate place in the Quadrant, readers will better understand how to successfully convey important messages to their listeners. The Skill and Will Quadrant is a must-read for communicators at any level.

Skill and Will Quadrant

Carolina Rodriguez

The Only Book you will ever need to communicate effectively
By Carolina Rodriguez
www.carolinarodriguez.co.uk

Published 2008 by arima publishing

www.arimapublishing.com

ISBN 978 1 84549 336 3

Printed and bound in the United Kingdom

Typeset in Palatino Linotype 12/14

Abramis is an imprint of arima publishing.

arima publishing

ASK House, Northgate Avenue

Bury St Edmunds, Suffolk IP32 6BB

t: (+44) 01284 700321

www.arimapublishing.com

To all those who want to understand the key elements of successful communication.

Acknowledgements

The author extends her special thanks to:

My husband Graham Thorn for his love that inspired me and gave me the strength and energy to pursue my dream, to my children Charlotte, Charlie and Michael who supported me and believed in this project, to Paula Pearson at Jenerator PR for her guidance, comments, and enthusiasm during this project, to Helen Tinner Photography, Patricia Arias and Melanie Lee for helping me to create the right image for this project, to Phil Baker and his team for professional competence and project leadership, and for his many excellent suggestions and guidance for helping me better understand the difference between writing and speaking, to my mother Marisol Gabaldon for unconditional love and emotional support, and to my sister Libsen Rodriguez for her interest and faith in this project and her love.

Table of Contents

The will of man is by his reason sway'd.
–WILLIAM SHAKESPEARE

Foreword

Who should be reading this book?

Have you ever wondered why there are certain individuals whom you understand better than others? Are there people in your life with whom you have no trouble communicating – and others who never seem to be on the same page with you?

You're not alone. Poor communication negatively affects the majority of people. Regardless of occupation, location, experience, or motivation, millions of people struggle with how to get their message across. Sometimes, a single person can feel like an enormous obstacle, but in other circumstances, you might feel like the whole room is against you.

If you've ever been speaking to a person, or group of people, and had the thought, "They're not even listening to me. I don't understand – why is this so hard?"

There's good news. You don't have to accept this situation. With the implementation of a simple tool, called the Skill and Will Quadrant, you can eliminate any obstacle.

First you must recognize that your listeners aren't the problem. By changing the way you communicate with people, you can reach every single person on a deeper level. Whether your listeners are bored, confused, over-excited, or in any other way distracted from the task at hand, you can address each one individually and with immediate success.

Effective communications skills are essential for success in all aspects of life. And though every job applicant lists "an ability to communicate well" as one of his or her best qualities, few are truly effective communicators.

Whether you are a manager, a business veteran, or an employee-in-training, the techniques and tips outlined in this book can help you improve your communication skills. The Skill and Will model will teach you how to clearly and directly project your message so that every listener understands. You will learn how to monitor and interpret verbal and nonverbal signals, ask questions to get the information you want, and evaluate your own development.

Most importantly, you will learn how to achieve greater happiness and success by integrating the Skill and Will model into your daily life.

This book is intended as both a personal self-improvement guide for individuals and a training tool for managers, directors, administrators, and supervisors. The techniques you'll explore can be successfully implemented in any size company, and in any industry.

The Skill and Will Model works for people who want to:

- Better communicate with employees, employers, colleagues, family, friends, and others
- Increase their awareness of the importance of communication
- Learn how to increase their perception capabilities
- Identify unique personal traits to better understand individuals
- Use communication to achieve personal and professional goals

I've been developing and practicing the Skill and Will model for the last five years, with impressive results. I'm now ready to share my discoveries and experiences with the world. I am confident that by increasing your communication awareness and improving your ability to reach and influence people, you can start to live the life of your dreams.

Introduction

Imagine you are a technician for a manufacturing company. Recently, a certain product has come off the manufacturing line with a high number of defects. Your department manager requests that you schedule a re-training session to inform workers of the problem and develop a solution.

You feel confident and excited about speaking with your colleagues. In fact, you not only have a list of possible solutions to discuss, you have developed a few suggestions to improve other processes in the plant. You tell your manager not to worry; you are certain you can guide the discussion, and the problem will be fixed quickly.

The day of the workshop you walk into the conference room with your laptop and a white board, ready to work. You welcome everyone, explain the purpose of the meeting, and survey the room for a response. Nothing happens, so you press on. When you finish, no one has suggested any way to fix the issue, so you ask, "Are there any questions?" A veteran of the company raises his hand and lets out a stream of criticism of your solutions. But the rest of the group remains quiet. The meeting ends unsuccessfully. Flustered and discouraged, you have no choice but to report to your manager that the meeting was a failure.

Immediately you blame the other employees. How dare they treat you with so little respect? At least you tried to come up with something! The only person who spoke up had nothing but complaints! Why wouldn't they cooperate with you?

What you don't realize is that this group was not an unruly gang of troublemakers or simply too lazy to care. Each person in that room was experiencing something different. One person was afraid that the meeting was about lay-offs, and so chose to stay quiet. Another was resentful that she had not been asked to lead the group. The veteran who challenged you on every point was angry about changing so many policies, and the others had various levels of stress, boredom, and other feelings with which to cope.

As the speaker, your job was to identify these different states of emotion and address them. In order for your listeners to get the message, they must be motivated to listen. To motivate them, you must figure out where they are emotionally at that moment, and gently guide them to an emotional and psychological state in which they will be receptive to your message.

Although this situation is stressful, imagine yourself on the other side of the equation. You are a junior supervisor, and your superior has asked you to attend a quality management workshop. You aren't sure why you were chosen – are you sufficiently qualified? You wonder if you are the right person for the job, and if you really want to give up a Saturday to attend the training.

You arrive at the conference room and find a spot near the front, hoping proximity will force you to focus. The instructor begins lecturing about a method called the Six Sigma approach. He refers to several slides, sketches some charts on the board, and shares a few examples. Everyone else nods as though they understand, but you feel lost.

Two hours into the workshop you look down and notice that you've written very little. In fact, you have no idea what's being discussed. During the break you listen to your peers discuss the new method. You are starting to make sense of everything, but still feel frustrated. When the training resumes you take a seat in the back of the room. Rather than ask for help, you decide to give up. This training probably isn't necessary, anyway.

You return to your supervisor with very little to report. Embarrassed by your failure, you blame yourself. You just don't have the skills to be responsible for such complex information. Or maybe you should have tried harder. You've never been a good listener, and now the whole department has to suffer. One thing is certain; you will never agree to attend a training workshop again.

Here we have another example of how poor communication can hamper progress. You might be perfectly qualified to attend and report on the workshop, but you lack both confidence and motivation. Inadequate communication on the part of the instructor has exacerbated that fact, trapping you in a cycle of low will and low skill.

Another typical example of the negative cycle is education. Not all children have the same capability of understanding. Those who cannot adapt to the teacher's method of communication develop a lack of confidence and motivation. Rather than being attributed to poor communication, the child's low will and low skill are blamed on the child's weak abilities.

Whether you are trying to send a message or interpret one, poor communication can prevent success. Regardless of your role in the interaction, developing perception and adjusting your communication to reach every individual is essential to achieve your objective. This is the basis of the Skill and Will Quadrant communication methodology. Fully understanding and utilizing this concept can change your life. *It changed mine.*

The Realization

There have been difficult moments in my life where I couldn't understand why the situation I was going through at that moment was so uncomfortable.

One of my first experiences with real frustration occurred when I was a young teenager in Venezuela. I was working with a French travel operator as a tour guide, and I loved my work. As I guided tourists through the country, I was filled with the energy of a typical 19 year old. I had an insatiable hunger for life, and a tremendous will to travel and discover the most beautiful and exotic places in the world.

I was driven by a strong will to succeed. Unfortunately, my strong will was placing me in situations I was ill-equipped to handle. I did not have the knowledge or skills to entertain the tourists, understand their needs, and manage the accounts, reservations, and budgets. I was stretching myself too thin, my energy was diminishing, and I felt less and less motivated. I was losing my confidence and my enthusiasm.

My once very high will to do the job was deteriorating, replaced by a desire to quit. Waking up every morning to go to work became an unbearable chore. I had moved very quickly from a highly motivated individual to a person with extremely low will. And I had no idea how or why this change had happened.

If I only knew then what I know now...

I have since learned that we are not static individuals. Instead, we move between different states depending on various will and skill factors. What's more, the transition from one state to another can be a gradual or immediate shift.

Learning this fact of human nature did not happen overnight. Had I woken up at nineteen and realized the truth, I would have saved myself a few more years of frustration. Instead, my later work experience helped to further develop this line of thinking.

The Beginning

For five years I worked for American Express, developing and teaching managing and technical skills. Eventually, I became a software program manager. Part of my training included the Six Sigma methodology. Six Sigma is a methodology that focuses on process and technology improvements to reduce costs and streamline processes and production.

At the time I lived in the UK, and recognized that the majority of UK companies hadn't significantly developed a Six Sigma approach. As I had become a Six Sigma Master Black Belt specialist, I realized there was tremendous opportunity for me as an independent consultant. So I left my position at American Express and founded my own consulting company *Quality Manager Solutions* to deliver quality consulting services and train other corporations on the benefits and how to implement Six Sigma and improvement methods.

I worked with administrators and employees in a wide range of industries. I helped develop quality management solutions for professional financial services providers, telecommunications firms, banking institutions, government offices, and media companies. Regardless of the type of business, my services and workshops provided a set of tools to help companies define processes, identify problems, analyze results, define possible solutions, and strategize about how to improve.

But no matter how useful the tools, or how well I presented the information, I felt like something was missing. I knew that I was sharing a valuable message, and I genuinely believed that my workshops held practical benefits for those who attended. Yet I still found engaging my listeners to be difficult. I did not know how to motivate the group or influence change without generating complaints.

After some time, I started to understand that though my communication techniques were generally effective, they failed to address the individual needs of each listener. A project manager who presents the same information in exactly the same way to five different individuals cannot expect identical rates of success. People learn differently, and a single lecture presented to a group will result in varying levels of retention and comprehension. I needed to learn how to focus on individuals within the group to make sure my message was being heard.

A workshop attendee introduced me to NLP, or (Neuro-Linguistic Programming) in the year 2000. NLP was developed in the early seventies by Richard Bandler and linguist John Grinder, and has been widely used by psychologists as a tool to influence behavioral change. Bandler holds a BA (1973) in Philosophy and Psychology from the University of California, Santa Cruz and an MA (1975) in Psychology from Lone Mountain College in San Francisco.

Based on the subjective study of human language, the goal of NLP is to influence decisions by manipulating emotions, beliefs, and internal representations. Today, NLP has been adopted by therapists, administrators, career coaches, and others as an effective approach to interpersonal communication training.

I started reading about NLP, and became fascinated by the use of language to influence human behavior. I was intrigued that a person's emotional state could be controlled, and that speakers could manipulate the psychological state of listeners to achieve a desired result. I attended all the NLP courses offered by Richard Bandler until achieving my master certification in 2004. This study led me to the Skill and Will model of communication.

I did not invent the model. In fact, human resource professionals and other administrators had already begun developing this approach by the time I became involved. Though others had already identified the human trend toward varying levels of motivation and skills, I wanted to explore further. I believed there must be an easier way to understand each person, and to categorize each one differently. I also wanted to learn how to move my listeners from their current levels of skill and will, to the levels that would help them become receptive to my message.

Take-Aways

There are two main points I must emphasize before moving forward.

First, the purpose of the Skill and Will Quadrant is not to help you bend people to your will. This method cannot, and should not, be used to attempt to *change* people.

The goal of this approach to communication is to help you better explain *why* your message is important for all of your listeners, to motivate them to listen, and to help them perceive change as an improvement to their personal situations, rather than an inconvenience.

Secondly, the most important aspect of learning this model is not the *what*, but the *why*. In other words, the model and its applications will be thoroughly explained, but I am more interested that you understand *why* this method is important, *why* this approach works, and *why* I believe so completely in its potential to bring about great change.

PART ONE -THE SKILL AND WILL QUADRANT

1 - Understanding Human Skill and Will

You may be asking yourself, *"What is will? How is it created? And how do we know we have it?"*

Human Will

"Will" has been defined by various dictionaries as:

> *The faculty of conscious and especially deliberate action*

> *The power of control the mind has over its own actions*

> *The power of choosing one's own actions*

> *The act or process of using or asserting one's choice*

> *Purpose or determination*

In more simple terms, will is our personal desire to do or not do a particular task or activity. Every human being is driven by will. Our survival depends on that motivation. In fact, the will to live is hardwired into our biology.

Hunger, thirst, exhaustion, fear, sensitivity to temperature, and the fight or flight response are all biological side effects of our inherent *will* to stay alive.

Only human beings in rare circumstances, such as those who suffer from severe depression, lack the will to live.

On a smaller scale, will guides our day-to-day activities. Some tasks have become habitual human behaviors because they are essential for life. We have few, if any emotional reactions to such activities, so they require minimal will. Most of us are indifferent to daily routines, including waking up, bathing, eating, going to school or work, returning home, resting, and so on.

There are other tasks that we really enjoy. We have a strong desire, or will, to do these activities, even when they might be inconvenient or cause conflict. An employee with a strong will to golf on the first warm day of the year will skip work despite the consequences. A teenager with a desire to have the latest styles will spend mom's money without regard for the cost. A strong will is a powerful force.

But will is not just the motivation to *do*; will can be a desire to avoid, as well. We all have responsibilities we'd prefer to neglect. Many people lack the will to exercise or eat properly, even though they understand the health effects. Some of us have a terrible time getting motivated to get up earlier than usual, or attend a potentially grueling meeting.

Will is not necessarily a static psychological state of being. Will drives a human being to do or act in a very specific way in a very *specific time*. If an individual has a lifelong will to avoid eating meat, he or she will probably maintain that motivation long-term. However, our will can change from moment to moment.

While you might not be motivated to attend a meeting at five a.m., your will might shift if the meeting is shifted to five p.m. and there's a promise of a catered dinner. Or, a child who is motivated to clean his room by the promise of £5.00 will lose his will if that incentive is revoked.

Will can shift quickly. Our desires and motivation fluctuate from moment to moment. Often, a simple change of plans can shift our motivation. A few words from another can change our position. The transition is nearly imperceptible to the untrained observer, but with instruction and experience, anyone can learn to recognize an individual's level of will, and initiate a transition.

Human Skill

Skill is defined as:

> *An ability, coming from one's knowledge, practice, or aptitude to do something well*
> *Competence in performance*

Expertness

A craft, trade, or job requiring dexterity or special training

Proficiency, facility, or dexterity acquired or developed through special education and experience

An art, trade, or technique

A developed talent or ability

Skill, for being an evident and substantial quality, is easier to define than will, which is primarily a core set of intangible feelings. From the moment we are born, our survival also depends on our ability to learn. We come into this world with a will to live, but without the skills necessary for survival. We must be taught. And the skills we learn as infants stay with us into our adult lives.

As children we learn skills as they are needed. Without even realizing it, our parents teach us what we should know based on an informal hierarchy of needs. First we learn life skills, including feeding ourselves, using the bathroom, dressing ourselves, and tying our shoes. We learn to stay close to mom or dad, how to avoid pain, and how to get attention.

Next, we learn social skills. We get our lessons on "Please" and "Thank you." We are taught how to share and take turns, and how to be kind to others. We learn not to interrupt another person, how to appropriately ask permission, and how to otherwise exercise self-control.

Instruction about colors, letters, and shapes is our introduction to academic skills. Upon entering school, our social and academic skill sets greatly increase.

Eventually, we choose hobbies and career paths that lead to the development of very specialized knowledge and talents. But throughout our lives, we continue to add volume and improve in all skill areas.

Like will, skill is a variable human characteristic. In a given circumstance, an individual might possess an insufficient, adequate, or excessive level of skill. Also, that level of skill can increase or decrease, depending on changes in a situation.

A professional trained in the Skill and Will model can effectively manage any group of individuals by identifying each person's unique skills, along with his or her level of skill in certain relevant areas. By appropriately utilizing the skills of each member of the group, the Skill and Will model allows all participants to feel necessary and valuable, thus increasing their receptivity to new information.

The Interdependent Relationship between Skill and Will

Skill and will exist independently of each other; however, they are also deeply entangled. They significantly affect one another, and are in a constant state of interdependent flux. Consider this example of how skill and will can directly impact each other:

An entrepreneur came to me for guidance. Her business was not succeeding at the level she had expected, and she could not figure out what she was doing wrong. I asked her to explain her personal level of motivation.

"I'm very excited about my business," she said, "I work very hard to improve every aspect. I have big plans for the future. I am really, really, motivated to do well, and I'm willing to do whatever is necessary to reach my goals."

This particular individual has a very high will. So I asked her to discuss her feelings about her *ability* to make the business work.

She responded, "I make really great plans, lots of useful lists, but when it comes down to it, I feel overwhelmed by the amount of work. I read as much as I can, and research all of the areas where I feel inadequate, but there's so much. I really don't know what I'm doing most of the time."

I asked her how this feeling of inadequacy affected her motivation.

"It's very, very discouraging," she admitted, " I get so behind, trying to learn skills as I go, that I just feel tired and disappointed in myself. I usually give up on a task before I finish. I never complete those great lists I mentioned before."

This woman's low level of skill significantly impacted her level of will. Without a will to improve, she was unable to acquire the skill she needed. She was locked in a perpetual cycle of failure, despite her initial enthusiasm.

My advice in this case was to tackle one skill at a time. I explained that the best option was to choose one area that needed improvement, master that skill, complete the task, and only then move on to the next objective. By following this routine, my client was able to change the direction of her skill and will pattern.

When she felt extremely motivated to complete an objective, she focused her energy on educating and training to reach that goal. Acquiring a valuable new skill and completing a challenging task led to increased motivation to approach the next obstacle. The perpetual skill and will cycle was reversed for a more positive result.

In this simple, but ever-changing relationship, an individual's will is controlled by his or her level of skill.

Inversely, one's level of skill is driven by personal will. The optimum goal is to maintain a high level of both skill and will. Skill and will specialists have learned to take advantage of the flexibility of the skill and will relationship. They teach that, by making an adjustment to either side of this equation, we can produce positive results.

In coming chapters we'll discuss how such adjustments can be made in both your personal and professional life through the use of effective communication tools and the power of personal conviction.

2 - Blanchard's Situational Leadership Model

The *Blanchard Situational Leadership Model* is the best known example of situational leadership theory. In the 1960s, Ken Blanchard, a management expert, worked with Professor Paul Hersey to develop a method of management called, *Management of Organizational Behavior*. The approach teaches leaders to evaluate the needs in a particular situation and assume the most appropriate style of leadership. Like other models of situational leadership, the Blanchard model is based on two concepts: management style and development level.

An Early Prototype

Because of its simplicity and utility in all areas of business, the Blanchard's Situation Leadership model is the most popular method of situational leadership training. Generally used in the corporate world to teach new managers about situational leadership skills, the aim of the model is for leaders to understand how to most effectively manage employees and to recognize the gaps in employee training.

For example, the Blanchard model teaches managers to recognize *why* an employee is not performing well. If a task is assigned to someone and the job is not sufficiently completed, the failure can most likely be attributed to one of the following reasons:

> The task has been delegated to someone who is unwilling - or unable - to complete the job. That individual has therefore decided to remain relatively uninvolved or "hands-off."

> The task was over-explained to a competent person. If a manager is too directive or "hands-on" with a person who is quite able to complete the assignment without assistance, the employee becomes very unmotivated.

Therefore, learning to appropriately adjust your style of interaction is essential to success as a manager, coach, or leader of any situation.

The Skill/Will Matrix

The Skill/Will matrix was designed to help managers decide how to manage individuals. The matrix, which is based on these two factors, is used to weigh an individual's strengths against his or her weaknesses. To be effective, a manger must carefully evaluate an individual's level of motivation (will) and training (skill). By cross-referencing these traits on the matrix, a manager can determine if the employee is capable of handling tasks independently or if he or she needs motivation to complete specific tasks.

High Will	Guide	Delegate
Low Will	Direct	Motivate
	Low Skills	**High Skills**

Skill depends on training, knowledge, understanding, and role perception.

Will depends on desire to achieve incentives, security, and confidence.

The matrix is a simple graph on which one axis represents skill:

How much skill does the employee have to do their job?

Is the employee qualified?

Is the employee overqualified?

How much experience does this employee have?

When is the last time this employee successfully learned a new concept?

How quickly does this employee handle tasks compared to peers?

The other axis represents will. The manager asks the following questions to measure the employee's level of desire.

Does the employee like his or her job?

Are you certain?

Has the employee ever explicitly expressed personal job satisfaction or enjoyment?

Does the team view this employee as an energetic person?

When was the last time this employee generated a really innovative or useful idea?

Does this employee participate actively in meetings?

Is this employee attentive during discussions?

Does this employee EVER talk?

Does this employee talk ALL THE TIME?

Accounting for Change

In *Blanchard's Situational Leadership Model* this graph is not used as a precision instrument. There is no precise mathematical formula to categorize employees into specific segments. Rather, the comparison matrix is a tool that allows the manager to better formulate a *general impression* of an employee.

The matrix has some use, but I believe some adjustments are necessary for this method to be truly effective. If a manager is allowed to administer direction based on a *generalized perception* of an employee, he is overlooking a vital aspect of the skill and will model.

An employee's overall personality and capabilities consist of far more than his or her level of motivation and training at any given moment. The employee might fit into a certain category now, but in a matter of time, that position will change.

Let's say that a High Will/Low Skill rating is assigned, and the manager assigns the employee's full-time job based on that result. The manager has "stamped" the employee as a particular type, and will permanently interact with and delegate to that employee the same way. This approach might work once in a while, but eventually that High

Skill/Low Will person will transition to another level, perhaps one of Low Skill/High Will. This change was not anticipated, and will therefore go unnoticed and mishandled by the manager.

Managers who do not appropriately and regularly adjust their leadership styles will constantly and consistently push employees in the wrong direction. This lack of attentiveness and flexibility is what causes miscommunication and misunderstanding. The results can be disastrous.

The matrix is a good place to start, but managers must be trained to recognize the dynamics of change in each individual.

A Better Long-Term Solution

My version of the situational leadership model is not a matrix. Based on my understanding that individuals are not quantifiable or constant, I have developed the *Skill and Will Quadrant*. The quadrant represents four distinctive skill and will states of being. As we experience different situations in our lives, we move from one quadrant to another.

The fluid transition from one quadrant to the other can happen over time, or in a matter of seconds. The secret is to understand where an individual fits into the quadrant *at the moment you are communicating*. If you can identify the individual's current level of skill and will, you will know exactly how to communicate with that person. You will understand how to adjust your language and behavior to achieve the positive behavioral change you need from the other person, and you will prime that person to *hear your message.*

Evaluation and adjustment must occur every time you interact with an individual.

3 - The Skill and Will Quadrant

I first experimented with the quadrant when I was running a repetitive series of training courses for a car manufacturing company. The one-day training course was designed to teach employees how to utilize a set of tools to improve certain areas within the business. The training was delivered across the company to more than 150 employees over a period of three months.

During the initial workshops, I realized that not all of the training participants were willing to listen or receptive to the information being presented. Naturally, I felt very frustrated. I was expelling so much energy to share knowledge that I believed had real worth, but I just couldn't seem to get my message across. That's when I decided that I would have to change my approach.

I considered the lack of response I had experienced in the first workshops. No one was interested, everyone looked bored, and the level of enthusiasm was dismal. I knew that I had to find a way to quickly and powerfully change the energy in the room. If I could get the attention of my listeners right away, I would stand a better chance of communicating my message throughout the training.

But how can you get the attention of an entire group of people who obviously have no will to be present or participate?

That question is impossible to answer. A speaker might manage to get the attention of a reluctant group of people, but *maintaining* a level of 100% engagement is impossible.

Based on my experience and study of the **Situational Leadership Model,** I realized that I could not change the will of the group by addressing them as a single entity. I needed to reach each person individually. And once I made that personal connection, I needed to make that person understand *why* my message mattered *to him or her.* Each employee had to recognize that the information I was presenting had *personal* significance.

If my listeners could individually justify the training, they would be more likely to accept the changes I was proposing.

In short, you simply cannot communicate a complex and complete message to listeners unless you appeal to each one independently.

With that consideration in mind, I drafted my first version of the Skill and Will Quadrant. Though similar to the Situational Leadership Model Matrix, the quadrant provided me with greater flexibility. Even in its earliest form, the quadrant allowed me to evaluate the *immediate* level of skill and will for every person in the room.

High Will		
Low Will		
	Low Skills	**High Skills**

Armed with my quadrant, I needed to find an efficient way to assess the participants.

Key Questions

I decided my approach would be most effective if I could capture the interest of the group within the first ten minutes. So I developed a set of questions that I believed would give me the diagnostic information I needed about each member of the group.

The Key Questions were as follows:

> *Please introduce yourself.*

What department do you work in?

What is your role in the department?

What position or job did you hold previously?

How long have you been with the company?

Have you ever been involved with a business improvement program?

Why are you here, or why do you think your presence was requested in this training?

The interview process averaged about five minutes per person, which was manageable. As each participant answered my questions, I noted responses and body language. Before moving on to the next person, I placed the employee in the appropriate segment of the Skill and Will Quadrant.

These questions worked well in this particular situation, but they can be adapted to any training circumstances. Though specifics may change, the relevance of the questioning process remains the same.

The Key Questions should:

- Set the tone for the training
- Break the ice

- Establish an open and accepting environment
- Acclimate participants to your personality
- Introduce the purpose of training
- Familiarize the participants with each other
- Unify the group

and most importantly:

- Help you determine each participant's level of will (enthusiasm, motivation, energy level, and purpose)

- Help you determine each participant's level of skill (training, knowledge, experience, ability to learn and take direction, and unique talents)

I should mention that your role as researcher should be played discreetly. Do not announce to your listener(s) that you will be carefully evaluating responses and categorizing individuals according to levels of motivation and training. Key questions should be incorporated into your usual group introductions. The idea is to warm up the group and make everyone comfortable, while learning as much as you can about each person's skill and will. Approach this process casually, but do not forget your objective.

Key Questions can also be adjusted to accommodate one-on-one or personal circumstances. Remember that the purpose is to figure out how the individual is feeling in the moment. Any subsequent interaction must reflect your understanding of the other person's emotional and psychological position.

Case Studies

The introduction of the Skill and Will Quadrant yielded fascinating and *useful* results. The following case studies illustrate how responses to the Key Questions translated into viable data I could use to customize my training style.

John (JS)

> **Please introduce yourself.**
> My name is John Simmons.
>
> **What department do you work in?**
> I work in the product design.
>
> **What is your role in the department?**
> I run the Quality Management areas.
>
> **What position or job did you hold previously?**
> Before coming here, I worked in GE for five years running the quality department program and implementing improvement projects.
>
> **How long you been with the company?**
> I've been in the company for about four years.
>
> **So, you have experience in quality management and business improvement?**
> Yes, quite a lot.

Why are you here, or why do you think your presence was requested in this training?

I'm responsible for our improvement programs. I guess I'm here to find out if there are tools or techniques I don't know about yet. I'm looking forward to getting the latest information so this company can run as smoothly as possible. (he laughs) I think we would all like that.

I considered John's answers. First I evaluated John's level of skill: John mentioned several years of experience in quality improvement. He had overseen the implementation of several improvement projects and currently had a high level of responsibility regarding quality management.

I knew that John was definitely going to feel very comfortable with the training subject matter. He would most likely be familiar with many of the concepts I was introducing. John was a classic **High Skill** participant.

Next, I considered John's level of Will: John knew his stuff, perhaps better than anyone in the room. I would have to manage him carefully, because an industry veteran might be a bit resistant to someone else's approach. There was a possibility that he would disagree with some of my methods, because he probably had his own effective improvement techniques.

However, John had expressed enthusiasm about expanding his knowledge and improving the company. He would be an ideal participant to involve in examples, and would openly share his own experiences with success and failure. If he remained receptive to change and modest about his expertise, John's leadership experience would benefit the entire group. Because he came eager to learn, I categorized John as High Will.

This is how John fits into the Skill and will Quadrant:

High Will		JS
Low Will		
	Low Skills	**High Skills**

With the next example, I want to show that the Key Questions are not limited to a rigid format. They can be blended into a single "tell us about yourself" introduction. The response will still give you enough information to make an informed decision about the individual.

Tony (TK)

I posed this statement to Tony:

Would you please introduce yourself, and tell us a bit about your career and history with this company. Also, what do you hope to gain from this experience?

Tony responded:

My name is Tony King, and I have been with the company for more than 12 years. I started as a technical assistant when I left college and moved through the organization in different roles. I now head the development team. I've worked in numerous improvement programs over the last ten years, and I've not actually seen any meaningful improvement so far.

Tony's response was short, but packed with useful information. I examined Tony's level of skill first: Tony had been in the company for more than twelve years. I judged that he had extensive knowledge of the business, processes, and tools in the organization – definitely High Skill.

I had another expert on my hands, but a very different personality to manage. I assessed Tony's level of will. He mentioned that he had worked in numerous improvement programs, but felt they were fairly useless. He didn't appear to be very keen on the idea of yet another training program. He had no reason to believe that the tools I had to offer were really going to help. For this reason, I placed Tony in the Low Will category. His final evaluation looked like this:

High Will		
Low Will		TK
	Low Skills	**High Skills**

I had to pay special attention to this participant, because he could become very negative during the training. I anticipated that he would be reluctant to get involved with the exercises that I had planned. I also knew that, due to his previous negative experiences, he might challenge me on my methods.

However, I knew I could manage Tony if I could figure out a way to improve Tony's attitude, like placing him in a group with highly motivated individuals or asking him to share his professional opinion or suggestions about how to approach a particular problem. I could leverage his experience and use Tony as a valuable resource throughout training.

In the next chapter, we will outline specific strategies to help you manage individuals from each placement in the quadrant.

4 – Using Skill and Will to Get the Best from Your Audience

For the purpose of this chapter, I will discuss how to use the quadrant when managing a group of people. Remember that these techniques can also be applied to personal relationships and one on one conversation, which we will discuss later.

Recognize, Interpret, Manage

The key to utilizing the quadrant is identifying the strengths and weaknesses of your listeners or participants. Once defined, the listener's personal traits - both talents and impediments - can be leveraged for optimum use. Every individual in the group can contribute; in fact, for the experience to be productive, every individual in the group *must* contribute.

Your job as the leader is to dismiss all of your preconceived notions about the group. We are human, and therefore inclined to judge others quickly and without in-depth analysis. Your first impression of the group is important, because you will be carefully analyzing body language and other behaviors. However, be aware that any negative response you have toward an individual must be eliminated. To do that, the individual's behavior must be *recognized, interpreted,* and *managed.* For example:

Recognize

Cynthia walks into the conference room. She is nursing a cup of coffee and hasn't removed her sunglasses yet. She appears disheveled, and annoyed. You greet her warmly; she nods, takes a seat in the back, and takes out her cell phone. You *recognize* that Cynthia obviously does not want to be here – her will at this moment registers as low, but her skill is yet to be determined.

Your first inclination will be to react negatively towards this kind of behavior. However, you have been studying the Skill and Will Quadrant, and understand that this behavior is indicative of a deeper problem. Rather than ignoring Cynthia and her low will, you decide to *interpret* the behavior.

Interpret

You observe Cynthia throughout the group introductions, and gently ask her the Key Questions. She responds with quiet and short answers.

When asked, *"Why are you here today?"* Cynthia answers, "I'm *just* an administrative assistant - a substitute for the person who was *supposed* to be here. A good friend of mine. She was fired Friday without warning. It's not fair, but whatever. I'm here now. "

Now you have gotten to the root of the problem. In a rush of words and emotion, Cynthia has explained why she is so angry. True, she does not want to be here, but she is not resentful of you or the other members of the group. She is harboring powerful negative emotions about her company's managerial staff, but probably feels indifferent about this workshop. Instead of avoiding the black cloud Cynthia has brought into the room, you have interpreted her behavior and understand *why* she is demonstrating low will.

Manage

Your next step is to devise a way to *manage* Cynthia's behavior. She doesn't want to be here because a) she is upset about the decision to fire her friend b) she probably doesn't feel qualified to handle the material and c) this workshop was dropped on her just one day before, and she was forced to cancel plans. So, what do you do with this?

Furthermore, Cynthia's level of skill still remains in question. She is an administrative assistant, so her specific skill set is unlikely to relate directly to your message; however, she may have talents that could aid in your presentation. As such, Cynthia falls in between a low skill/low will and high skill/low will classification.

If you intend to engage Cynthia in your presentation and share the importance of your message, your next step must be to both direct and motivate her.

First, Cynthia's negative energy must be redirected. As you strategize about the roles each participant will play in this workshop, you must define a special function for Cynthia. She must become an active participant, and she must see value in the information, or your message will be lost.

You learned from her responses to the Key Questions that she has experience with administrative tasks. During the first small group session, you pull Cynthia aside and explain:

"Cynthia, you've probably noticed that this group is mainly comprised of folks from the product engineering department, and I understand that you are an administrative assistant with your company. As you know, when things go badly on the production line, managers are quick to place blame. You've probably been on the receiving end of some misplaced anger, right? I've been there myself. My goal here today is to make sure that doesn't happen again. If everyone works hard today and pays attention, production will really improve, and your managers will relax. So, here's what I'm asking from you: This group has many strengths, but they might need some help staying on task. I think your organizational and multitasking skills will really come in handy today. Would you be willing to help me? "

You have genuinely empathized with Cynthia. You have motivated her by identifying why she should be personally invested in the workshop, and she feels understood. You have also directed her. You ask her to assist with collecting and organizing information from the groups. Cynthia sees the value of her presence and agrees to help.

By the end of the day, Cynthia has taken on a leadership role. Without prompting, she has assumed responsibility and expedited many of the administrative tasks that usually slow down the workshop. By performing a necessary function, Cynthia has developed a personal sense of purpose. Inadvertently, she has also learned the vital information that the workshop was intended to convey.

With careful management, Cynthia has been transformed from low will/low skill to a willing and well-trained participant. You have successfully moved Cynthia to a high skill/high will placement within the quadrant.

Managing Individuals at Different Skill and Will Levels

The Skill and Will Quadrant was designed to help communicators learn how to best connect with their audience members. To succeed, leaders must first carefully recognize and interpret an individual's level of motivation (will) and training (skill). This will help the communicator place each participant in the quadrant and, more importantly, understand *why* he or she falls into that specific category.

In the simple but ever-changing relationship between skill and will, an individual's will is controlled by his or her level of skill. Inversely, a person's level of skill is also dictated by his or her level of will. The objective of the Skill and Will Quadrant is to identify specific strategies to improve and maintain a person's level of both skill and will. By managing participant's skill and will, communicators can better transmit their message and emphasize the importance their message has for the participant.

Part of managing participants involves determining if each person is capable of handling tasks independently or if they will need motivation and encouragement to stay involved. As you'll recall, the Skill and Will Quadrant is not a method for *changing* people. Instead, the Skill and Will Quadrant is tool designed to help communicators and managers prime their audience to hear a message.

The Skill and Will Quadrant provides specific strategies for communicating with individuals in each quadrant.

High Will	Guide	Delegate
Low Will	Direct	Motivate
	Low Skills	**High Skills**

The Low Will and Low Skill Individual

An audience participant with a low level of will and skill requires special attention. This person does not have a great deal of skill to understand nor the will to try and comprehend your message. A person with low skill and low will needs direction.

As the communicator, you must be able to *direct* the low skill/low will participant in order to aid her in seeing the importance of your message. This person will need a lot of direction from you. She does not have the skill to identify the importance of the communication on her own, nor does she have the will to make an effort.

The important thing to remember when dealing with a low skill and a low will individual is that placement in the quadrant is not static. Just because that person has a low skill and a low will at that place and that time does not mean that she is always lacking in skill and will altogether.

Recall Cynthia from the previous story. Cynthia had skill and will; however, the skill and will was not focused on my presentation or message. By directing Cynthia, I was able to overcome her low skill and will levels, involve her in the presentation, and transmit the importance of my message – all without her ever realizing that she had changed.

I directed Cynthia by:

- Demonstrating how her participation could benefit her
- Making use of her available skills in a constructive manner

The High Will and Low Skill Individual

A high will and low skill individual is lacking specific knowledge but possesses a strong desire to learn. The best way to manage a high skill, low will individual is to *guide* that individual through the process.

Remember: human skill and will directly affect one another. The biggest obstacle to effectively communicating with a low skill and high will participant is the possibility that her lack of skill will frustrate her and decrease her will. If you lose this participant during the session, that person's low skill level will directly affect her will to learn. The objective of the communicator is then to transmit information to the low skill, high will person in a way that she can understand.

A high will, low skill person will need to use her high will to compensate for the lack of skill. This person must be guided and given the tools to learn and use other people's skills and knowledge. You must offer guidance and make certain that the participant is following along with your message – without making your concern for the ability to keep up noticeable.

The objective of the skill and will quadrant is to effectively communicate your message with participants – and whenever possible, move the participant to a higher placement in the quadrant. If possible, the high will, low skill person should be guided to a higher skill level throughout the course of the training.

One way to manage a high will, low skill person would be to have another participant with a high level of skill share his or her information with the participant with the lower skill level. This strategy relates directly to the Opponent Quadrant, which is outlined in Chapter 6.

The Low Will and High Skill Individual

An individual with low will and high skill has the know-how to complete a task or understand a message; however, that person's will is not directing them to make the effort. A person with a high skill and low will requires *motivation* to move them toward the next level: high skill and high will.

High skill/low will individuals require as much, if not more attention than individuals with low skill and high will. Participants absolutely must be motivated to comprehend and understand your message; otherwise the thrust of your communication will be lost.

If you cannot inspire motivation in this type of individual, you will not be able to utilize their talents (skills) to your advantage during the presentation or emphasize the importance of your message.

The high skill and low will individual also presents a threat to the rest of the participants. If he chooses to be negative, his bad attitude can seep out and contaminate other participants. The low will of any individual must be actively managed.

Motivating low-will individuals in a group setting might seem like a daunting task, considering that motivation comes from within an individual. However, identifying, assessing, and interpreting each person individually can make motivating even the most low-will participant much easier.

There are two factors which motivate people most:

1. Fear of loss
2. Desire to gain

During the process of asking Key Questions, recognizing, and interpreting, you must accurately assess the *why* of the person's low will level. Is that person lacking motivation because he or she has been stuck in the same dead end job for the last 10 years?

A person such as that has neither fear of loss nor desire to gain – no motivation whatsoever to make the effort to understand your message. In a scenario like this, you must strike at the participant's desire. Identify a way in which understanding your message would benefit the participant. What could he or she gain from participating in the communication?

For instance:
- Increased knowledge
- Greater efficiency
- Praise from the higher-ups
- An opportunity to establish themselves as an expert in a specific field

Alternatively, you might also attempt to stir up the participant's fear of loss. What might he or she lose if they fail to understand your message? Their job? Their chance at a cushy promotion? The opportunity to learn a valuable new skill? Identify something of value that the audience member could lose by failing to participate.

Personally, I prefer using desire to gain as a motivation tactic. Desire to gain is a positive motivator, and the majority of people respond better to positive stimulus. Fear of loss should only be used as a motivation tactic when all other avenues have been exhausted.

Another way to motivate a high skill, low will individual is to use their skills to your advantage. The high skill person has knowledge in areas that other participants with lower skill levels might be lacking. Consider Tony King from the previous chapter.

Tony has more than 12 years of experience with his company and falls easily into the High Skill category. However, Tony also expressed doubt at the importance and relevancy of my message. He didn't demonstrate any desire whatsoever to participate in another training seminar. Tony's will to participate was low.

A team member like Tony had the potential to become very negative during the training. High skill, low will individuals are often reluctant to get involved and may challenge the authority of the speaker. To motivate Tony, I involved him in the group by requesting that he share his expertise with the other participants. By actively managing Tony's low will level, I was able to leverage his experience and use him as a valuable resource in my training.

The High Will and High Skill Individual

A person with high skill and will has both the ability and desire to learn. The biggest obstacle for communicators dealing with a high skill/will participant is in keeping the participant in tune with the message and maintaining his levels of skill and will.

One of the best strategies for managing a high skill and high will individual is to delegate tasks to him. Ask him to lead a group exercise or share his expertise with the other participants. Make use of this person's talents and then delegate some of your authority to him. People often learn best through teaching, so delegating responsibility to a high skill/high will individual will benefit both parties.

First, learn from and listen to this person so that you can then communicate on his frequency. When you are both tuned to a comfortable channel, you can then share the merits of your message and ask him to help educate and guide the other members of the audience.

5 - Interpreting Human Behavior

The Key Questions will open the door, but to lead effectively, you cannot rely solely on listeners' responses to your questions. There are far too many variables at play to depend on words as your only source of data. In every circumstance, you will have to rely on subtle behavioral clues to accurately assess each individual.

Some of us are better than others at recognizing and deciphering signals. Many people have used their inherent ability to understand, empathize, and relate to others to achieve success in business and in life. For that reason, the ability to interpret human behavior can be considered a talent.

However, behavior interpretation is a *learnable skill*. With sufficient training and experience, anyone can learn how to better recognize and interpret verbal and nonverbal signals to accurately assess the emotional, physical, and psychological states of others.

The following participant scenarios reflect circumstances that we have all experienced in some capacity. Whether you have served as the leader of a group or just participated in a discussion, you will recognize these personality types.

The Enthusiast

The majority of the time you will be dealing with professionals who are totally comfortable discussing their background and expectations. Some will probably share a little too much. If you encounter such an individual, consider yourself lucky and watch for subtle body language.

The Liar

Although we would like to believe that participants are always completely open and honest, the fact is that they aren't. Occasionally, a participant will embellish or omit details. This is usually done to impress others or protect information the individual views as sensitive.

The Liar in a group will say one thing, but his or her behavior will tell another story. You must learn to read between the lines to discern the truth about this person.

The Dodger

The dodger persistently evades a responsibility. This participant, for reasons we will discuss later, is reluctant to speak. Reponses will be very short, usually just a few words. Dodgers do not volunteer information; you will have to ask very direct and detailed questions to get what you want. Body language will be a primary source of information. This kind of behavior usually indicates low will. Listening for voice tone will help you discern *why* this person is unwilling.

Non-Verbal Signals

Of all the species, humans have the most complex system of non-verbal communication. Before language, we relied only on physical signals to share messages. Even though early human speech eventually evolved into the intricate and diverse languages we know today, we have retained our ability to send and receive physical signals.

We are all involuntarily sending and unconsciously interpreting a universal code of physical expressions. In fact, this ability is instinctual, and therefore imperceptible to the untrained observer.

Outward behaviors are clear signs of an internal monologue. You cannot know what an individual is thinking, but you can be fairly accurate in your estimation if you know how to interpret behavior. There are several physical indicators you should note as an individual speaks, including posture, facial expression, arm position, movement, focus, and breathing.

Posture

Posture is indicative of several non-verbalized emotions and attitudes. Stiff, erect posture can mean the participant is nervous, closed off, defensive, confrontational, angry, afraid, or otherwise uncomfortable.

However, some people tend to sit up straight when they feel very confident and at ease. Tone and other clues will help you determine a particular individual's state.

Facial Expression

Most people demonstrate their level of stress by frowning or furrowing their brows. Look for these signs of tension, as well as pressed lips, clenched teeth, and wide eyes. On the other hand, a relaxed expression, easy smile, and soft eyes let you know that the individual is comfortable.

Arm Position

Most behavioral experts agree that folded arms usually indicate defensiveness or anger. However, many people fold their arms across their chests when they feel totally relaxed. Do not take folded arms as a warning sign; the speaker might be extremely laid back.

Arms and hands flat on the table signal to others that this person is in control. This behavior tells you the speaker is confident – perhaps overly so – and used to being in charge.

Hands in pockets, when sitting or standing, are a sure sign of nerves or feelings of inadequacy.

Hands on hips, like folded arms, demonstrate either aggression or extreme confidence. Watch for other clues to determine between the two.

Movement

Movement refers to pen or finger drumming, foot tapping, leg shaking, and any other repetitive behavior. Fidgeting can mean one of two things: the speaker is nervous, or the speaker is bored.

Keep asking questions. If the speaker is bored, the responses will be short, and delivered in monotone. If the speaker is simply nervous, your gentle line of questioning will help him or her to calm down and open up.

Focus

Where is the speaker looking? Where he or she chooses to place focus can tell you a lot.

If the speaker maintains eye contact with you, or addresses the group, he or she is comfortable and confident.

On the other hand, an individual who focuses on anything but you and the group is probably feeling nervous and uncomfortable. Continue to engage the person; warmth and attentiveness will draw his or her focus away from a notebook or table and up to you and the group.

Eyes cast down, as described above, indicate nerves or disinterest, but a speaker who can't seem to focus on anything in particular might also be experiencing discomfort or boredom. Wandering eyes, staring into space, and rapid glances all indicate low will, regardless of the speaker's words.

Breathing

Here's a tip: If you notice the speaker's breathing, assume he or she is uncomfortable in some way. A content and relaxed individual will breathe normally, even during speech. A person who is nervous, afraid, angry, or distracted will breathe in unusual patterns.

You might observe sighing or short, quick intakes of air. People experiencing boredom will often use loud, deep breaths to express this feeling, but unusually long inhalations are also a sign that a person is having difficulty calming down or focusing. Abnormal breathing is subtle in most cases, and almost undetectable in others, so watch carefully.

Specific Body Language Clues

Here are some common behaviors of which you should be aware:

Sitting with legs uncrossed, apart: open and relaxed

Hand to cheek: contemplating, attentive

Touching nose: deceiving, doubting

Touching eyes: stressed, doubting

Hands behind back: angry, superior, anticipating

Crossed legs with locked ankles: nervous

Head tilted: attentive, interested

Preening: insecure, nervous

Hands clasped behind head: superior, disinterested

Head in hands: bored

Nail biting: nervous, disinterested

Pointing: confronting, accusing

The Body Language of Deception

In my experience as a trainer, lying is a rare occurrence. I do not expect that you will have to actively seek out and identify the deceivers in a training group. And in most cases, participants who choose to lie are not doing so out of maliciousness. The majority of the time, an individual chooses lying only as a method of self-protection or self-defense.

A person might lie to compensate because he or she feels inadequate. Or, the lie is told to cover up some aspect of the person's history that he or she doesn't want to share with the group. Whatever the reason, you can only place an individual in the quadrant and develop an effective training strategy if you know the truth about his or her levels of skill and will.

Learning to recognize and address deceptive behavior will also help you handle other relationships, whether business-related or personal. Deceptive behavior is easily spotted if you know what to expect.

Typically, a person who is lying will display very stiff, restricted behavior. A liar is subconsciously trying to take up as little space as possible, so hand, arm, and leg movements are limited and close to the body. They might touch their faces and mouths often as they speak, or place an object between themselves and you as a subconscious symbol of separation. But individuals with the intent to deceive will rarely use gestures that traditionally express sincerity, such as a hand over the heart or face-up, open palms.

Eye contact, or the lack thereof, is also an obvious indication of deception. A lying individual will avoid eye contact, usually by directly looking away or casting, wide, dramatic glances about the room.

Look for a long glance to the right. Creative processes generally occur in the right hemisphere of the brain, and a person fabricating information will tend to glance in that direction. The left hemisphere is responsible for memory, so if a person glances to the left while speaking, you can safely assume the lack of eye contact has more to do with nerves or insecurity.

Also, take note of which hand is dominant. If the speaker is left handed, but gestures or touches the face with the right hand, this is a sign that the creative side of the brain is at work.

Be aware of timing and contradictory behavior. If a physical expression of an emotion lasts longer than seems natural, or is suddenly stopped, the behavior is probably forced. Deception is probably taking place if a physical action is delayed until after the verbal expression, such as a big smile that follows seconds after the statement, "I'm really happy to be here."

Verbal Signals

In addition to body language, behavioral psychologists have studied what the human voice can reveal about our internal state. Even when we try to control our behavioral signals, our voices betray us.

The words your participants use to express themselves are crucial, but the manner in which those words are spoken can be equally telling. Speed, volume, pitch, coherence, cadence, and tone are clear indicators of an individual's emotional and psychological condition. Pay attention to these factors to uncover the hidden agenda (or reduce the apathy) of your participants.

Speed

Rapid speech could mean that the person is nervous or excited. Fast talkers are usually anxious about their level of skill, or very motivated to participate.

An individual who talks slow is usually either insecure in his abilities or unwilling to become engaged. Generally, you can assume a slow talker is searching for the right words to appear competent, or bored and unwilling to expend much energy crafting a thorough response.

But how can you tell if the person is demonstrating true skill and will levels or if he or she is just a naturally fast/slow talker?

To determine if a person is speaking at an abnormally fast or slow rate will take some preliminary surveillance.

Observe how the individual interacts with others before engaging him or her in conversation.

Assessing speed will be easier if you have an example of the person's normal speech for comparison. If the individual naturally speaks quickly or slowly, you will have that information and ahead of time, rather than assuming the rate is based on a particular level of skill or will.

Volume

Like speech rate, most people maintain a consistent level of volume when comfortable. Again, you will need to determine whether your participants naturally speak softly or loudly by observing or engaging them in discussion prior to asking Key Questions.

Volume tends to rise when a person feels agitated or energized. If a subject is speaking abnormally loudly, he or she is nervous, excited, or very confident. People also speak louder than they usually do if they feel pressured to prove themselves. They either feel they must fight to make themselves heard, or so competent they believe they should be leading the group.

Quiet voices either get lost in the crowd or intensely command attention. Low volume from a person who normally speaks at an appropriate level is a sign that the person is nervous, bored, or lacks confidence. This is indicative of low will and/or low skill.

Pitch

Pitch fluctuates when powerful emotions are present. Unnaturally high pitch or rapid and erratic changes are the results of increased adrenaline. In fact, vocal control is directly affected by physiological reactions like a rise in blood pressure or temperature.

If a speaker's voice seems unnaturally pitched, assume this person is extremely nervous, afraid, angry, or otherwise agitated. Occasionally, a speaker will demonstrate low will by involuntarily lowering voice pitch.

Coherence

Is the speaker making sense? A calm and collected speaker will organize his or her thoughts well and demonstrate a clear purpose. This could mean you are dealing with a high will/high skill participant.

If the speaker appears confused, is unable to follow a train of thought, or fails to make a point, the incoherence can be attributed to nerves or boredom. Garbled speech or otherwise poor communication is associated with a low skill and/or low will individual.

Cadence

Cadence refers to the speaker's rhythm and pace. Consistency is associated with confidence and comfort.

Like erratic pitch, sporadic changes in speed, sudden or long pauses, and a general absence of vocal restraint means the person is experiencing very strong emotion. Nerves, insecurity, fear, or anger is likely the cause.

Tone

This is the vocal characteristic people are most comfortable interpreting. During our earliest skills training, we learned how to recognize sarcasm versus sincerity, excitement versus boredom, and comfort versus anxiety.

Some participants will intentionally use tone to nonverbally express an opinion, but many speakers are unaware of the signals they are sending via their tone of voice. You will innately recognize blatant verbal signals, such as an angry or hopeful tone, but make sure you are dialing in to the more subtle cues as well.

The Verbal Language of Deception

If your interview subject gives you false information, you'll know. Here's how:

The use of formal speech is your first warning sign. For example, if the speaker avoids contractions he or she is trying to cover misrepresentations of the truth. "I don't know" is probably true, but "I do not know" could be an overblown attempt to appear genuine.

Highly technical language is also used to compensate when a person feels insecure or inadequate. People pad their résumés; they also pad their conversations.

If you swing the pendulum the other way you'll recognize another signal of deception. Ambiguity is just as indicative of lying as overly-specific language. Speakers who talk a lot without really saying anything significant might be using avoidance to cover the truth.

Excessive speech, even when relevant, also suggests lying. A person who is lying will assume that pauses imply fabrication. He or she might talk more to cover the silence and mask any lies.

Some liars will use someone else's words to cloak their deceptions. If a participant answers questions by throwing your exact words back at you, take those responses with a grain of salt.

Finally, a person who wants to deceive you might speak in incomplete phrases or omit pronouns. People generally like to get credit for their successes. If responders speak in short phrases or avoid using the words "I" or "me," they could be lying. Your comprehensive understanding of verbal and non-verbal clues will deeply enrich your assessment process. Combined with the responses you accumulate, your interpretation of behavior will allow you to construct an accurate and multi-dimensional image of each person.

Profound insight will help you precisely place each individual into the Skill and Will Quadrant and subsequently build an effective communication strategy.

6 – Opposites Attract

"Opposites attract" is a law of nature. Because of its intrinsic connection to human behavior, this concept also applies to the Skill and Will Quadrant.

As you develop new methods of utilization, you will assemble a dynamic list of techniques to apply to the quadrant. The "Opposites Attract" principle can be successfully implemented in almost any circumstance. Nearly universal application means you will employ this principle often, so this is the first of the behavior management tools you should master.

In physics class we learned the basics: negative (-) is attracted to positive (+) and vice versa. Opposites attract. The study of energy transmission tells us that all energy in the universe exists and transfers according to polarity and the laws of attraction.

We have all witnessed how this broad theory can apply on the much smaller scale of our daily existence. Many human relationships succeed because the parties involved are very different from each other. Consider the unlikely couples who seem to click, despite their obvious lack of similarities.

Relationships can survive, and in many cases thrive, when the people have little or nothing in common. Have you ever asked yourself, "What does she/he *see* in him/her?" If you can't easily answer such a question, you are likely witnessing a powerful force of nature in action: opposites attract.

How is this possible?

Opposites attract because the universe seeks balance. Like all of nature, human beings are in constant search of equilibrium. All of us have strengths and weaknesses, likes and dislikes, passions and repulsions, fears and motivations, talents and imperfections, and a thousand other human characteristics. What we lack, we subconsciously search for in others. We seek out companions who fulfill our needs, who make us whole. The best partnerships are those on which one personality compliments the other.

The Skill and Will Quadrant takes advantage of this principal by pairing dissimilar individuals. In most situations, individuals with contradictory traits work well together. When differing personalities collaborate, gaps are filled and deficiencies are overcome. When opposites are grouped together, the result is a single, blended entity. The aim of the Skill and Will Quadrant is to foster an environment in which every person is an active, enthusiastic participant. A variety of talents and perspectives working as one achieves this goal because collaboration leads to intense scrutiny and practical solutions.

The Opponent Quadrant

To utilize the "opposites attract" principle for the Skill and Will Quadrant, you must recognize the dynamics of the group. In time you will become skilled at identifying the level of skill and will of each person in the room. However, you must also understand that, for each individual in the room, there is another person with a very different personality. Every participant has a counterpart, an opponent, with polar opposite levels of skill and will. Pairing these opposing forces could result in a very productive match.

Once you have identified each individual and his or her opponent(s), you can generate a *Skill & Will Opponent Quadrant* to help you develop the most effective training, teaching, or communication strategy possible.

Individual	Opposite
High Will/Low Skill	Low Will/High Skill
High Will/High Skill	Low Will/Low Skill

Case Studies

Pairing High Will and Low Skill with Low Will and High Skill

In one of my Six Sigma training programmes, I used the Key Questions to determine how each member of the group would fit into to the Skill & Will Quadrant. Karl Jones and Laura Peters were participants in the workshop.

Karl's five minute introduction at the beginning of the training went as follows:

> "Hi, my name is Karl. I've worked in the operation areas of the company for three years. I recently moved into the reengineering department, so I look forward to the Black Belt Training. Coming from the operation areas, I can see how we can use the improvement methods to improve service performance."

Karl had a background in operations but had never been introduced to the Six Sigma methodology. As far as his understanding of production and quality improvement systems, Karl was not very skilled.

However, Karl was enthusiastic about learning a new skill. He was pervious, and believed that with this knowledge he could contribute to and improve his department.
After my initial Skill & Will Quadrant analysis, Karl (KJ) was categorized as High Will & Low Skill on the quadrant.

High Will	KJ	
Low Will		
	Low Skills	**High Skills**

Compare Karl's statements to Laura's introduction at the beginning of the training:

> "Hi, my name is Laura. I've worked in the reengineering department as a programme manager for the last five years. Previous to working in this company, I was a green belt in Six Sigma at Company X. The constant changes in the organization of the goals and training programmes have made it very difficult to apply sustainable improvements and benefits. Honestly, I think Six Sigma doesn't work well in this organization."

Laura had already been formally trained in the Six Sigma methodology in her previous company. Her Green Belt certification meant she was qualified to implement and manage various improvement projects. Laura was highly skilled.

However, past negative experiences had affected Laura's perception of the methodology. She did not believe the system could work, and saw little chance for improvement. She was not motivated.

Based on her introduction, Laura (LP) was categorized as Low Will & High Skill.

High Will		
Low Will		LP
	Low Skills	**High Skills**

Here were two individuals with very different backgrounds working in the same department. Different paths had led them to the same destination, and with the same goal in mind. Both participants were attending the Black Belt Training to find ways to improve production, but there was a significant variance in their individual levels of skill and will. They were, in fact, opposites of each other. They were opponents on the Skill & Will Quadrant.

	Low Skills	High Skills
High Will	KJ	
Low Will		LP

To achieve my goal of effective communication, contrasting levels of skill and will could not be disregarded. I needed to bring balance to these two people, and ultimately the entire group. I recognized an opportunity to pair these opponents. By working together, they would both benefit from training:

1. I asked Laura to coach Karl on the new methodology. By acknowledging Laura's advanced skills and giving her responsibility, I was able to gradually increase her level of enthusiasm about the methodology.

2. I asked Karl to use his experience in operations to find solutions. At the same time, his enthusiasm about the methodology would positively influence Laura. By explaining how and why he thinks the approach will work, he could transform her opinion.

The result of this combination was a smooth transition for both parties. Propelled by Karl's positive energy, Laura shifted from a low will to a high will individual during the training. Experiencing a different perspective helped her to find value in the training. Laura's newfound understanding of *why* his information was important allowed me to successfully communicate my message to her.

Karl, under the guidance of a skilled professional, progressed from low skill to high skill. Karl had tremendous enthusiasm, but lacked sufficient knowledge. Left on his own, or paired with an equally inexperienced partner, Karl would have struggled to keep up. Laura's expertise and leadership were integral to Karl's success. Her coaching supplemented Karl's workshop training, allowing him to fully comprehend and absorb my instruction.

A partnership forged between opponents resulted in balance and successful communication.

Pairing High Will and High Skill with Low Will and Low Skill

This scenario may be trickier to manage because the High Will & High Skill individual will be more assertive than the Low Will & Low skill individual. Balance is difficult to achieve if one person dominates the other. However, with guidance from you, each partner can complete a vital function in the team without overpowering or submitting to the other.

The following example illustrates this kind of combination.

Barry Lewis (BL) was a participant in one of my training workshops. He had years of experience in change management and statistics and improvement programmes. He had recently been promoted to Operations Director in an insurance company and was keen to develop a strategy for his IT infrastructure improvement programme. He was attending the workshop to learn about how the combination of two methodologies, ITIL(the IT Infrastructure Library) & Six Sigma, could help.

Barry was a textbook High Skill and High Will participant.

High Will		BL
Low Will		
	Low Skills	High Skills

Darren Walker (DW) and Tom Lane (TL) were present in the same workshop. Darren and Tom were employees of the same company. Due to restructuring in their department they were attending the workshop to satisfy new job requirements. They appeared to share the same negative attitude.

An obvious lack of interest and experience in improvement programmes indicated that they should both be categorized as Low Skill and Low Will.

High Will		
Low Will	DW TL	
	Low Skills	**High Skills**

Managing this volatile combination required finding a balance between widely disparate levels of will and skill. In order to be effective, I had to figure out how these opponents (Barry and Darren/Tom) could compliment and help each other.

I encouraged Barry to help during the workshop by facilitating some of the exercises and activities. I split the group in half, taking care to separate Darren and Tom. I lead one group, and Barry assumed responsibility for the other.

One low will person can be challenging, but when two unmotivated people team up, the negative energy they generate can be detrimental to the success of the workshop. Their cyclical negativity would eventually spread to others in the room. Misery loves company. Fueled by Darren and Tom's low will, the entire group would eventually turn pessimistic.

Separated from their partner in crime, Darren and Tom couldn't help but change their attitudes. Fast preventative action eliminated a potentially destructive force.

Combining these opposites resulted in the following benefits:

1. This arrangement provided a break in the cycle of negative energy between two Low Will and Low Skill personalities

2. I was able to gain control over the influence of Low Will individuals on the group

3. I had an opportunity to fulfill the expectations of a High Will/High Skill person by giving him hands-on experience leading and managing a team

4. I was able to provide Low Skill/Low Will individuals with personal attention and interaction with a motivated and skilled team member. This allowed them to recognize the value of the information and derive inspiration from the expert's enthusiasm.

5. I had more time available to manage the Low Skill/Low Will personalities in the room.

6. Low Skill/Low Will individuals were able to increase their knowledge and actually enjoy the workshop.

Summary of Steps

1. Identify where the individual fits in the quadrant using Key Questions.
2. Pay attention to each participant's body language and verbal cues to reaffirm placement in the Skill and Will Quadrant.
3. Identify whether Skill is driving the will or vice versa
4. Recognize, Interpret, and Manage each individual based on his or her specific needs
5. Identify an opposing force for each individual - the opponent.
6. If possible, group the individual with an appropriate opponent(s) for all activities.

7. If an opponent doesn't exist within the group, make sure the individual does not pair up with someone who has matching levels of skill and will. In this situation, you should take on the role of the opponent and partner with the individual.

PART TWO - PERSONAL APPLICATIONS OF THE SKILL AND WILL QUADRANT

7 – Communicate Effectively by Identifying Channels

How many times have you tried to change someone's mind or convince others of something that you believe is true? We all have our own way of communicating - and generally, we use the same method throughout our daily lives, without taking into account how others might perceive our message. We simply say what we need or want and do not take the time to understand how our listener is processing the information.

Sometimes this approach works well, but more often, this kind of communication leads to disaster. One-sided communication is frequently to blame for misunderstandings, hard feelings, and even heated fights.

Wouldn't our lives be happier if all of our attempts at communication were successful? Wouldn't we experience more peace if we were able to accurately exchange information without disagreements over simple misunderstandings?

Well, there is a way to make this happen.

First, aim to synchronize with your opponent on his or her "channel." Too often we try to force our opinions on others. We concentrate too much on convincing others to see a situation our way, and not enough on understanding their unique perspectives. We get so wrapped up in trying to influence our opponents. We forget *why* our message is important and *how* we can most effectively communicate that message.

Imagine that each person has a unique communication style, like a personal radio channel. You might believe that your style of communication, or channel, is the best, or "right" way to share information. But, if we only broadcast our messages on our own channel, we fail to reach the listeners who are tuned in to other channels. In order to be heard, we must adapt to the communication style with which our listeners are most comfortable. We must synchronize our channel.

Adjust your Frequency

Consider this example:
Veronica and Alex are planning a weekend vacation; Veronica likes swimming, fine food, and long walks on the seafront. Alex is a more dynamic individual who prefers to spend the weekend surfing, indulging in fast food, and drinking a couple of beers in the evening.

These are two very different individuals, with very different ideas about what constitutes relaxation and entertainment.

Usually, in this type of relationship, one of the partners will take on a more submissive role. Because this partner wants to please the other, he or she is more willing to compromise, and usually complies with the more dominant individual's preferences. This situation may not be sustainable, however, because the compliant partner is putting more into the relationship. He or she is working harder and sacrificing more than the dominant partner. Eventually, the submissive individual in a relationship will start to feel resentful of his or her partner.

In the case of Veronica and Alex, assume the weekend vacation is Veronica's idea. Her dilemma is figuring out how to approach Alex with her plans so that he is interested in joining in Veronica's favorite activities. How can she approach the subject in a way that makes Alex feel excited about the vacation, rather than resentful or disappointed that he has to give up his idea of fun to please Veronica?

Veronica employs her typical approach in this situation: *"Darling we need a weekend away. Wouldn't it be nice to go to a beach resort for the weekend so we can relax and spend time together?"*

Because he cares about Veronica, Alex's reaction could be, *"Yes, of course,"* when he's really thinking, *"Next time I will go with my friends for a real weekend away."* If he's not up to the compromise, Alex might reply, *"Sorry Darling, I've got too much work this weekend. Maybe another time."* Given Alex's adverse response to Veronica's vacation style, that time will probably never come.

Veronica needs to understand and synchronize to Alex's frequency, so she can share her thoughts and receive a positive response.

A more effective approach is:

"Alex, when was the last time you had an ideal weekend?" Alex searches his memory. He recalls the time and place of his last perfect weekend vacation. His body language and psychological state immediately start to change. He feels relaxed and open.

Alex has tuned in to a frequency to which Veronica can relate.

Veronica continues:

"Tell me, what was so good about the weekend? What did you do? What did you eat?" Alex goes into detail about his memory, essentially outlining a descriptive guide of his preferences.

Now that she knows what would make Alex happy, Veronica can take advantage of the shared frequency to propose her plan for the weekend.

"Alex, wouldn't it be nice to go away next weekend, both of us? What you're describing sounds wonderful. We can experience those same things together. In fact, we can do all of the things that you and I enjoy so much - like beach walks and surfing, great food and fine drinks..."

At this stage, Veronica has successfully communicated to Alex that she would love to go away with him. Alex is more likely to be enthusiastic, because he can now connect Veronica's suggestions to his previous, very positive experience.

You might perceive the tactic used in this example as manipulation, but Veronica did not exploit Alex or the situation. Most importantly, she did not try to influence her opponent with deception, complaining, begging, or other negative communication strategies. She simply adapted her communication style - not to gain the advantage - but to communicate more effectively with Alex. There is a saying in chess: ***Play the board, not the player.*** Veronica focused on communicating her message, not on persuading her partner.

Leverage Interest and Agreement

The example of Veronica and Alex illustrates a crucial point: the situation can change dramatically if you are keenly aware of w*hy* and *how* you want to communicate a message.

One way to successfully influence your opponent or partner is to identify and leverage areas of mutual interest and agreement. As a professional consultant, I've seen this approach to communication work successfully many times. When one party sincerely strives to understand the perspective of their opponent, they naturally change their own point of view. This human tendency to adopt our opponent's opinion is a very powerful phenomenon - one that proves we are all capable of understanding and flexibility.

8 – Dealing with Conflict

The Skill and Will Quadrant provides an excellent tool for managing and overcoming communication conflicts in both professional and personal environments.

When people become emotional about an issue, they tend to lose perspective of the problem and the situation. At that point, stepping back from the dispute and reclaiming control of the situation can become difficult. In order to communicate more effectively in a potentially controversial situation, you must learn to accurately assess the situation *before* the communication process begins.

What Causes Conflict?

Conflicts can arise whenever people – whether close friends, family members, co-workers, or romantic partners – disagree about their perceptions, desires, ideas, or values. These differences can range from the trivial, such as who last took out the garbage, to more significant disagreements which strike at the heart of our most fundamental beliefs and concerns. Regardless of the substance of the disagreement, conflict often arouses strong feelings and emotions.

Disagreements can lead to both parties feeling angry or hurt and for many people, feeling hurt places them into a sense of vulnerability. People generally feel less "in control" when they have been wounded emotionally in a dispute. This loss of control can then manifest as anger in an attempt to regain power.

About Anger

Anger is one of the greatest threats to the healthy resolution of conflict. Anger leads people to say and do things that they would not normally do, especially when they are already in the midst of a conflict. Use of the Skill and Will Quadrant can help prevent and diffuse tension and anger in a conflict.

It is important to note that feelings of anger are not an issue if the anger is channeled and handled constructively. Anger is a normal human emotion – an emotion just as natural and healthy as joy, happiness, and sadness. Anger becomes problematic when it prevents the resolution of a conflict that could otherwise be solved in a reasonable manner.

Communication Ground Rules to Avoid Conflict

1. Remain calm.

   Try not to overreact to difficult situations. A calm demeanor gives your viewpoint credibility.

2. Express feelings in words, not actions.

   Telling someone directly and honestly how you feel can be a very powerful form of communication. If you start to feel so angry or upset that you feel you may lose control, take a "time out" and do something to help yourself feel steadier - take a walk, do some deep breathing, pet the cat, play with the dog, do the dishes - whatever works for you.

3. Be specific about what is bothering you.

   Vague complaints are hard to work on. Give the other person specific suggestions of areas he or she can improve the situation – and ask for them to suggest improvements for you as well.

4. Deal with only one issue at a time.

   Don't introduce other topics until each is fully discussed. This avoids the "kitchen sink" effect where people throw in all their complaints while not allowing anything to be resolved.

5. No "hitting below the belt."

   Attacking areas of personal sensitivity creates an atmosphere of distrust, anger, and vulnerability.

6. Avoid accusations.

   Accusations will cause others to defend themselves. Instead, talk about how someone's actions made you feel.

7. Don't generalize.

Avoid words like "never" or "always." Such generalizations are usually inaccurate and will heighten tensions.

8. Avoid "make believe."

   Exaggerating or inventing a complaint - or your feelings about it - will prevent the real issues from surfacing. Stick with the facts and your honest feelings.

9. Don't stockpile.

   Storing up lots of grievances and hurt feelings over time is counterproductive. It's almost impossible to deal with numerous old problems for which interpretations may differ. Try to deal with problems as they arise.

10. Avoid clamming up.

    When one person becomes silent and stops responding to the other, frustration and anger can result. Positive results can only be attained with two-way communication.

Conflict is a normal, inevitable, and even healthy aspect of most relationships. When managed well, conflict can actually be used to enhance and strengthen relationships with friends, family members, co-workers, and romantic partners. The Skill & Will quadrant provides you with the tools and techniques to help you achieve positive results when problems arise.

Place Your Objective and Your Opponent in the Quadrant

I use this particular method when dealing with individuals that have previously proven to be difficult to talk to and communicate with.

Before you interact with a quarrelsome person, ask yourself, "What is the purpose for this interaction?" This paves the way for a more effective conversation.

Once you have clearly identified the purpose or a goal for the interaction, then you should clarify that objective in your mind and begin the process of placing the individual in the quadrant versus your goal. How might that individual's skill and will affect the likelihood of achieving your objective?

If you are unable to identify a clear purpose for the conversation, then the best thing to do is step back and let the conversation dissolve in simple ideas and the exchange of thoughts. If there is no purpose for the conversation, there is no reason for conflict to arise.

Imagine a scenario in which you are facing your yearly evaluation with your boss. You know his budget is tight, but you more than earn your keep and would like to demand a salary to match your responsibility. What do you want to be the end result of that meeting? If your objective is to obtain a generous raise (and not lose your job), consider the boss' skill and will in relation to your salary.

- Determine Skill
  Does your boss have the authority and/or funding to give you a raise?
- Determine Will
  Does your boss believe you deserve the raise or have a desire to reward you for your efforts (will)?

High Will	**Your Opponent** Your Boss	**Your Objective** A Raise
Low Will		
	Low Skills	**High Skills**

In the fore mentioned scenario, your boss has a high will to give you a raise. He knows that you've earned a reward, and would like to give you a competitive salary increase. However, his department's budget is tight and he doesn't have money to make more than a modest increase to your income.

In this scenario, you must find a way to move your boss from a level of high will and low skills to a level of high will and high skills. Because you've prepared for the conversation and identified your opponent's Skill and Will in relation to your objective you will be better placed to negotiate. For instance, you could point out ways in which you directly increase the department's profits.

I often use the Skill and Will Quadrant in conversations with my ex-husband. In the past, we have entered into difficult fights due to a lack of understanding and inability to clearly communicate on both ends. To diffuse potentially explosive conversations, I aim to ask him questions to mentally identify where he sits in the Skill and Will Quadrant.

For instance, imagine how I might prepare for a conversation with my ex-husband about spending money on the children. In this scenario, his will, or his *desire* to or not to spend money is more important than his will, or his *ability* to spend money. My goal for the conversation would then be to establish the level of his will or his budget for the particular scenario. How much money is he willing to spend?

> Me: *"Hi. I'm calling you to discuss the children's upcoming holidays. There are a few weekly clubs available to keep them entertained. Have you given their holidays any thought?*

Now I have expressed my thoughts and given him the opportunity to share his thoughts.

Him: *"No, I haven't had time to think about it yet.*

Me: *""OK, no problem. As I said before, we have a few options. I just need to know what your budget is so we can make choices about which holiday clubs to send them to."*

I have now determined his budget, or his will to spend money. Even if he is low will in this case, he will still give me some figure to work with and use as a starting point for future negotiations.

This technique can be used in almost all potentially conflictive communications. Taking a moment to pause and clarify your object will help avoid future miscommunication, conflict, and anger with your family, friends, and colleagues.

9 – Master the Art of Communication

Can you think of a conversation that you have been putting off for some time? You know you should talk to someone, but keep postponing the conversation. We procrastinate for a number of reasons: nervousness, fear of rejection or anger, or lack of confidence.

Maybe you've tried previously and the discussion went badly, or maybe you fear that talking will only make the situation worse. Regardless of the cause, there's a feeling of being stuck, and you know that wasted energy could be spent more productively.

Below I've summarized some of the best strategic questions. This is a checklist of action items to think about *before* communicating, concepts to consider *during* the conversation, and some tips to help you stay focused and receptive. These suggestions will also help you identify possible openings in a conversation. You'll notice a common theme throughout:

You have more power than you think.

How to Prepare for the Conversation

All of your anxieties about initiating the conversation can be assuaged if you know what questions to ask. Before going into the conversation, ask yourself:

1. **What is your purpose for having the conversation?** What do you hope to accomplish? What would be an ideal outcome? Be aware of hidden purposes. You may think you have an honorable goal, like educating an employee or building a relationship with your teen. However, you might notice that your language is excessively critical or condescending. Your intention is to support, but you end up punishing. Carefully examine yourself to make sure you enter the conversation with a positive purpose.

2. **What assumptions are you making about your opponent's intentions?** You might feel intimidated, ignored, disrespected, marginalized, or worse. But - be cautious about assuming that this was the speaker's *intention*. Impact does not necessarily indicate intent.

3. **Which of your "buttons" is being pushed? Are you more emotional than the situation requires?** Take a look at your "back-story." What part of your

personal experience is being tapped? Recognizing what emotional baggage you bring to the table means you'll enter into the conversation knowing that the heightened emotional state is partially caused by you.

4. **How is your attitude affecting your perception of the conversation?** There is such a thing as a self-fulfilling prophecy. If you go into the conversation expecting the process to be horribly difficult, you will probably have a terrible experience. If you truly expect success and believe good things will happen, that will likely be the case. You must adjust your attitude for maximum effectiveness.

5. **Who is the opponent? What might he or she be thinking about this situation?** Is he or she aware of the problem? If so, how do you think the issue is perceived? What are your opponent's needs and fears? What solution do you think your opponent might suggest? By putting yourself in your opponent's shoes, you can begin to make the transition from opponent to *partner*.

6. **What are your needs and fears?** Do you share any common concerns with your opponent? Should you?

7. **How have you contributed to the problem?** Are there specific mistakes or errors in decision-making

to which you should admit? Accepting some responsibility for the problem indicates to your opponent that you are not here to blame or accuse.

8. **How has your opponent contributed to the problem?** Can you explicitly define the role your opponent has played in the situation? You will need this information to support your case and seek a resolution.

The Five Golden Rules

In any conversation that has the potential for conflict, the majority of your energy will be focused on yourself. You will work harder to manage yourself than you will to influence your opponent. Even if the encounter begins well, you'll need to stay in charge of yourself, concentrate on your purpose, and direct your emotional energy. Remember to breathe and centre yourself. Constantly check in with your emotional and psychological state; if you become off centre, make a conscious effort to return to a balanced state. This is where your power lies. By choosing a calm, centered state, you'll help your opponent/partner to be more centered, too.

Rule #1: Use Inquiry to Zero in On Frequency.

In order to find out what channel your opponent is tuned to, you have to let him or her take the lead. Project an attitude of genuine interest and curiosity. Pretend you don't know anything, and try to learn as much as possible about your opponent/partner and his or her point of view.

To get started, assume your opponent is operating in a different world. You must tune in to the correct frequency to find out how things look in that world, how certain events affect your opponent, and what values and priorities exist in that world.

You'll also need to analyze body language. What does your opponent really want? What can you learn from your opponent's body language about what is *not* being said?

Let your partner talk until he or she is finished. Don't interrupt except to acknowledge or indicate understanding. Don't take anything your opponent says personally. Remind yourself that this conversation is not really about you. Instead, use this phase of the conversation to learn as much as possible about your opponent. Don't rush; you'll get your turn.

Rule #2: Acknowledge and Synchronize to Your Opponent's Frequency.

Acknowledgment means demonstrating that you've heard and understood your opponent's message. Ideally, you should have such a thorough understanding of the opposing viewpoint, you could argue in your opponent's favor. In fact, you should verbally reflect your opponent's complete argument back to him or her.

Explain what you've ascertained from the conversation - what you think your opponent is trying to say or what he or she expects from the conversation. Your opponent will not listen or change an opinion unless you indicate that you understand and are on the same frequency.

The key is to acknowledge everything you can, including your own defensiveness or other negative thoughts. For example, in an argument with a friend, I explained, *"I notice I'm becoming defensive, and I think it's because your voice just got louder, which makes me think you're angry. I'm not trying to persuade you in either direction. I just want to talk about this topic."* Acknowledging my feelings helped both my friend and I to re-center and continue in a more productive manner.

Please note:

Acknowledgment can be difficult if associated with agreement.

Keep the two separate. If your opponent says, *"This sounds really important to you."* that doesn't mean he or she agrees. Likewise, acknowledging your opponent's message does not mean you are going along with that decision.

Rule #3: Decide What to Communicate and Why The Message Has Value.

When you sense your opponent has expressed all of his or her points on the topic, you may take your turn. From your perspective, can you recognize anything your opponent might have missed? Make sure you clarify your position *without* minimizing your opponent's opinion.

For example: *"I can see how you came to the conclusion that I'm not helping in the project. Though I understand your argument, I have to disagree. When I work on the problems with the project, I'm thinking about its long-term solutions and success. I don't mean to be negative or critical, though I understand how you could think that I am. Maybe we can talk about how to address these issues so that my intention is clear."*

Rule #4: Work With Your Partner to Find a Solution.

Now you're ready to begin developing a solution. Continue asking questions; brainstorming with your opponent-turned-partner is the most effective and inclusive way to solve the problem.

Begin by asking your partner for a suggestion. *"What do you think we can do to fix this?"* Be prepared, because you might not agree with your partner's proposed solution. Whatever the answer, find something with which you agree and can support. Then build on that element.

If the conversation becomes adversarial, put the ball in your partner's court. Return to the inquiry stage: *"So we disagree about this solution; is there another option you have mind?"* Asking for your partner's point of view creates a feeling of safety and encourages him or her to engage. Conflict is quickly averted if you consistently surrender some control to your partner.

Rule #5 Practice, Practice, Practice!

This technique is not just effective in business or work environments. Inquiry and synchronization are essential to good communication in all of your relationships. Follow these steps whenever the opportunity arises. The art of communication is like any art– continued practice is necessary to acquire Skill and Will.

Points to Remember:

- ✓ What do you want to communicate?
- ✓ Why do you want to communicate?
- ✓ How do you want to communicate? (synchronization)
- ✓ On which channel is your opponent operating right now?
- ✓ Do you need to alter your opponent's frequency?
  If you understand and feel comfortable with his channel - NO. If you do not comprehend or feel comfortable, change the channel so that you also feel at ease.
- ✓ Start with the **What**. Follow with the **Why.**

In Conclusion:

❖ A successful outcome depends on two interdependent factors: your attitude and your language. Your attitude (centered, supportive, curious, and problem-solving) will of course influence what you say.

❖ Acknowledge negative emotional energy - yours and your partner's - and redirect these forces for a constructive purpose.

❖ Fully understand your purpose, and return to this focus in difficult moments.

❖ Don't take verbal attacks personally. Acknowledge the cause of the behavior and help your opponent/partner re-center.

❖ Don't assume your opponent/partner can see things from your point of view. You should always clarify.

❖ Practice! Rehearse the conversation with a friend before initiating the real one.

❖ Mentally prepare for the conversation. Think of various possibilities and visualize yourself handling them with ease. Envision your ideal outcome.

There are dozens of books about how to handle difficult, crucial, challenging, and important conversations. I recommend the following.

Crucial Conversations, by Kerry Patterson, Joseph Grenny, Ron McMillan, Al Switzler
The Magic of Conflict, by Thomas F. Crum.

Also, Richard Bandler, the co-developer of Neuro-Linguistic Programming (NLP) conducts NLP seminars and workshops that deal with this topic.

10 – The Power of Conviction

Some people have a remarkable, almost uncanny ability to lead, guide, or convince those individuals around them. These leaders can be found everywhere in our lives – at school, university, work, and at home.

When was the last time you came across one of these influential individuals? Have you ever been one of them? Would you like to know how to possess the ability to influence yourself?

Allow me to ask you another question. Do you stand up for what you believe in? Do you even know what you believe in?

The common trait of influential individuals is conviction.

The importance of conviction cannot be emphasized enough. Consider these famous thoughts on the power of conviction:

> *"What convinces is conviction. Believe in the argument you're advancing. If you don't you're as good as dead.*

The other person will sense that something isn't there, and no chain of reasoning, no matter how logical or elegant or brilliant, will win your case for you."

Lyndon B. Johnson

A leader has the vision and conviction that a dream can be achieved. He inspires the power and energy to get it done.

Ralph Nader

Using the Skill and Will Quadrant, you can learn how to harness the power of conviction and empower yourself to drive situations and convince others.

Each one of us is unique and possesses specific skills that we can share with the rest of the world. Some of us naturally have the skill and will to identify and fulfill our goals – objectives that make use of our talents. Others do not spend time identifying and understanding our skills or lose steam along the way and fall short of reaching our full vision and potential. In other words, we fail to fully develop our skill and will.

Adapt Your Skill and Will

In order to influence others and harness the power of conviction, you first need to be able to convince *yourself*. Your Will must be high. Your Skill level should also be high; however, if your Skill happens to be low, your Will level must be used to compensate for the lack of Skill. Your enthusiasm and empowerment will need to drive your convictions and enable you to learn to use other people's skills and knowledge.

High Will		Best Quadrant to Harness the Power of Conviction
Low Will		
	Low Skills	High Skills

Example

Imagine that you join a new organization. Your new boss would like for you to work with the team to come up with a comprehensive strategy to reduce the organisation's employee travel costs.

- You have never met your new colleagues.
- Your previous job was within the procurement department dealing with third-party companies, including service travel firms

- Your skill level in the travel service is high; however, your knowledge or the organization is low.
- Your will is also high; you are convinced that if your solutions are implemented, the firm will profit greatly and you will shine in front of your new boss

Your boss arranges a meeting with your new colleagues. At the meeting, you meet with:

Sam Prescott (SP): Project Manager
Sam has been with the company for five years in the capacity of project manager. She has been involved in the implementation of IT development projects. Sam's demeanor and attitude indicate that she tends to follow the lead of the other team members; Sam appears uninterested in brainstorming for the best solution, she appears to prefer to contribute to the end result.

Patrick Oliver (PO): Programme Manager
Patrick has been with the company for 10 years, running improvement programmes across the IT and Operations area. Patrick is clearly the team leader.

Martin Carr (MC): Project Manager
Martin has also just started with the company. He has previously worked as a Project Manager in a procurement department for another firm. Martin

seems anxious to do well in the new position and aims to impress his new peers.

After the introductions, Patrick Oliver takes the lead. As a Programme Manager, he wants the project to be directed in the same way as usual. You recognize that Patrick rarely faces resistance from the other team members.

You have an objective for the meeting: to identify a comprehensive strategy to reduce the organisation's employee travel costs. Your will is high, a successful plan could land you firmly in your boss' good graces. Your skill in the travel industry is high; however, your skill in regard to the new firm is low.

You now find yourself in a situation where you want to communicate your thoughts and convince Patrick and the rest of the team that your solution is the best approach.

You use the quadrant to help you identify the team.

Step One: Define Where Your Audience Fits in the Quadrant.

	Low Skills	High Skills
High Will	You MC	PO
Low Will		SP? PO?

Step Two: Identify the Audience Members You Need to Convince and the Ones that Will Not Resist.

As you can see, Patrick appears twice in quadrant. In both placements, Patrick is identified as having a high skill. With 10 years under his belt, Patrick knows how to get the job done. Patrick might have a high will – to do things his way. On the other hand, Patrick could have a low will to lead. He may or may not be willing to relinquish some control and authority to you without opposition. Where Patrick falls in the Skill and Will Quadrant at this moment (remember, position within the quadrant can change instantly) will be largely determined by your approach.

Martin is new to the company, so his skills are low. However, he is also anxious to impress and learn, so his will is high. Martin will likely be eager to be a part of a winning solution. If you can make your point well, Martin will not provide an obstacle.

Sam has been with the company for a number of years and is in a position of leadership, so her skill is high. However, her will to dispute is low. Sam's focus appears to be on getting the job done – after the decisions have been made. She is unlikely to offer resistance.

Step Three: Manage the Audience Members That Will Need Work

Your management approach to each team member will depend on his or her placement within the quadrant.

Patrick Oliver

Learn from and listen to this person so that you can then communicate on his or her frequency. Only when you are communicating with Patrick on a comfortable channel should you try to convince him of the merits of your strategy.

Sam Prescott

Identify why this individual's will is low so that you can convince the individual of the positives of your strategy. How will your strategy's positives outweigh the negatives (or in Sam's case, eliminate the apathy) that this person is focusing on?

Martin Carr

As discussed previously, a high will, low skill person such as Martin will need to use their high will to compensate for the lack of skill. This person must be given the tools to learn and use other people's skills and knowledge.

To achieve the best results from your meeting, you could first ask Patrick to spend five minutes explaining the company approach. Make Patrick feel comfortable with your infringement on his authority by tuning to his channel and requesting that he impart his knowledge of the company with the new team members.

You have now taken control of the conversation, and also likely gained respect from Martin, who will have benefited from Patrick's explanation.

Now that you understand the company's project management approach, you can then start explaining your strategy in a way that pertains to the company's current methods.

Step Four: Demonstrate your Conviction

Emphasize your experience and your success with your previous company. Leave no doubt in your audience's mind that you are capable of developing a strategy that will work for the company and reflect well on the team.

This will register with Patrick and Sam – both of whom would like to be a part of a successful team. Invite the rest of the team to participate by requesting their comments and thoughts. You may face some challenges from Patrick, but your personal conviction in your plan and your abilities should allow you to manage his resistance with ease.

Remember: the power of conviction is an unshakable belief in something without need for proof or evidence.

Do you believe in yourself?

11 - Using the Quadrant in Job Interviews

The Quadrant is about taking control and having conviction about the strength of your abilities. By being in tune with the behavior of others, you can easily steer any interaction to get what you want or need. This is especially true of job interviews.

An interview is a volatile situation, one in which two parties are subtly jockeying for position. Usually, the most dominant personality wins. However, when you are armed with an understanding of the Skill and will Quadrant, you can effortlessly control the conversation, even if your opponent is powerful.

Some job applicants believe the interviewer has all of the control. Most hiring managers would agree. But regardless of which side you are on during an interview, you must be in full control from beginning to end. If you are interviewing a potential employee, you must use quadrant skills to determine whether or not the applicant is appropriate and capable. If you are attempting to get hired yourself, you must use the same skills to impress the interviewer and land the job.

For the Interviewer

The purpose of an interview is for the personnel manager to determine whether or not an individual is suitable for a particular position. Part of this process is completed through analysis of the applicant's resume and experience. But the most valuable information is collected *during* an interview, when the applicant's behaviour can be observed and interpreted.

The hiring manager must speculate about how the individual would behave as an employee. How would this person respond in certain situations?

The only way to determine probable behavior with any accuracy is by obtaining a *sample*. The interviewer must ask questions that will cause a behavioral response in the applicant. Those responses will act as a basis for forecasting how he or she will behave in the future.

There is a major disadvantage to this process: the behaviour an applicant displays in an interview may be uncharacteristic. We discussed earlier how anxiety, fear, and other feelings of discomfort can dramatically affect our behavior, but there are other reasons you can't always trust the behavior of a job applicant.

First of all, job interviews are relatively short. An interviewee who wants to make a certain impression can modify his or her behavior for a short time. For example, a rather ponderous individual can appear to be quite dynamic if he or she has only to maintain that energy for half an hour. This is especially dangerous when an individual with low skill or will is able to project tremendously high will.

Hiring managers have been known to hire ill-qualified or unmotivated persons because they demonstrated enthusiasm in the interview. Also, individuals are not static. An applicant who reacts to a question in one way today might have a very different response tomorrow.

To appropriately use the Quadrant as a hiring tool, you must review the purposes of an interview. Job interviews are designed to help employers:

- Assess the candidate's suitability for the position
- Learn information about the candidate
- Positively represent the company to the applicant

How Can We Tell If A Candidate Is Suitable For The Position?

Some hiring managers make the mistake of choosing employees based on a vague definition of a "good person."

However, the objective should be to choose the person who is most likely to *succeed* in a certain job or range of jobs. The following list reflects the most common questions interviewees typically use to assess the individual:

- How would your friends describe you?

- Tell us about a successful project you worked on.

- Tell us about an occasion when you worked as part of a team.

- Describe a time when you had to handle a difficult customer or solve a tough problem.

- Have you ever had to organize an event? Describe how you handled the situation.

Keep in mind, when you use generic questions to assess an applicant, you have no way of knowing if the interviewee is answering honestly. Your decision will be based on responses that might or might not be true. This means you have to place a lot of trust in a person you are just getting to know. To avoid making the wrong choice, I recommend using the Skill & Will Quadrant in the interview. This is a more effective way to determine whether or not a candidate is suitable for the job.

The purpose of utilizing the Quadrant is to learn how an individual responds to certain situations. What is this person's *natural state* when confronted with:

1. A High Will, High Skill situation?

2. A Low Will, Low Skill Satiation?

3. A High Will, Low Will Situation?

4. A Low Will, High Skill Situation?

	Low Skills	High Skills
High Will		
Low Will		

To answer these questions and determine if the applicant is suitable for the job, you will look at two factors:

1. How does the applicant react to specific circumstances?

2. Is the applicant capable of transitioning easily from one quadrant to another?

Let's start with a scenario. Our company releases the following job description:

Senior Project Manager

An exciting opportunity exists in a leading international defense technology company for a Senior Project Manager. This business develops innovative technology-based solutions and products and provides support services for major government organizations and world-wide commercial companies. We are the leaders in this field.

The Senior Project Manager will have overall responsibility for the effective delivery of customer-facing projects with a portfolio of projects valued between £1m and £5m throughout the full lifecycle.

The Senior Project Manager will manage various projects from initial conception (including research, design, development, advice, and procurement) to equipment supply and commissioning. Potential applicants must demonstrate a proven ability to translate project guidelines into specified work packages.

The Senior Project Manager will be expected to negotiate and commit to the delivery. By managing cost, quality, and resources he or she will ensure that early milestones meet objectives and exceed customer expectations.

Key Requirements
To be considered, applicants must:
- *Demonstrate leadership.*

- *Have an ability to build and lead teams consisting of members from wide range of technical disciplines.*

- *Have an ability to build positive relationships with both internal and external stakeholders.*

- *Have an ability to effectively manage all resources to meet contractual obligations.*

- *Have strong customer focus.*

- *Have excellent communication skills.*

- *Have an ability to maximize and secure sell-on opportunities.*

- *Possess a strong drive for results.*

- *Be an effective influencer across all levels of the organization.*

- *Be able to improve efficiency of processes.*

- *Set up and implement new procedures within the division*

- *Manage contracts with third party suppliers.*

- *Have strong solution definition experience.*

- *Have solid team development and coaching skills*

In conclusion, we are looking for an exceptional candidate with High Skill to do the job and High Will to succeed.

Evaluating Interviewees

Mathew James was selected for an initial assessment interview. We reviewed his curriculum vitae and decided that he met our technical and experience requirements. However, we also needed to assess whether or not Mathew's capabilities to communicate and lead supported his impressive credentials.

The best way to get an honest response from an individual is initiate a test when he or she is not expecting one. To get the most accurate reading of Matt, we needed to catch him off-guard, before he had time to prepare his response.

As we waited for the elevator that would take us to the interview room, I decided to ask Mathew about his home and his trip to our offices.

As the elevator arrived, Mathew told me he lived an hour away from London in a small town near the M23. I asked, "How long have you lived there? Is it a nice place to live? "

The elevator door opened and Mathew very politely held the door and asked me to go first. Then he responded, "Oh, it's a beautiful town. We are an hour by train into London and major airports, and the town has all the essential services- shops, post offices, banks and some great pubs. My family moved from Manchester ten years ago. We love the town and our friends."

I asked, "How was your journey today?" Mathew mentioned that he took the 7am train to ensure that he had plenty of time, as he was not exactly sure of the building's location in London. He also mentioned that he was horrified by how many people where commuting and how hard it was to find a seat on the train this morning.

As he described his experience, I noticed a note of discomfort in Mathew's voice, and a sudden change in his facial expression. He seemed to be contracting the muscles of his face.

The elevator door opened. Matt exited first and waited for me to lead him to the interview room. As we walked, we continued our conversation. I asked about his method of travel for his previous job. Mathew's answer was not very positive. He mentioned that he used to drive two hours to his office every day and another two hours to get home, *if* there wasn't a lot of traffic.

As he spoke, Matt's facial expressions didn't relax, and his voice remained strained. In a matter of minutes, Mathew had transitioned from a smiling, pleasant individual to being grumpy and negative.

We walked into the room, and I took my seat. Then I asked Mathew to sit down. His response would give me an indication of his confidence and communication preferences. Social psychologists have learned that seating arrangements significantly affect interaction.

Mathew chose to sit directly across from and facing me. People who choose this position are more likely to be assertive during an interaction. They will comment more often and are more likely to respond directly to opponents than people who choose an adjacent position. Sitting directly across the table also indicates a greater sense of formality.

To continue using the Quadrant, the interviewer must assess the applicant *before* the interview begins. Based on his choice of position and attitude at this stage in the process, I recognized that Matt was feeling slightly uncomfortable.

So far I had learned:

1. Mathew likes quiet environments. He is most likely to experience success in a small, controllable, and calm atmosphere. I determined this aspect of Mathew's personality be analyzing his answers to questions about his home. When talking about his quiet neighborhood, Mathew reflected positive, calm energy.

2. Mathew dislikes crowds and long commutes to work – whether by train or car. Let's face it: who

does? But my main focus was Mathew's psychological and emotional states.

a. Did the change happen when Mathew was faced with something he disliked?

b. Did Mathew express himself with the same attitude when he talked about something he *does* like?

c. Was Mathew pleasant and communicative even after subject of commuting was introduced? The answer was NO. Mathew stopped being polite and positive as soon as I brought up commuting. He had allowed his emotions to control his behaviour.

As a project manager, Mathew would often find himself in unpleasant situations where he would not have the option of allowing his emotions to take over. I knew that Mathew's tendency to behave this way was not a controllable reaction, because he was not acting consciously. He was responding naturally to my questions. This was Mathew's normal behaviour.

3. Mathew prefers to communicate in a formal manner. When he sat across from me Mathew returned to a High Will state. He was comfortable with his position.

The assessment continued. Before I started the formal interview, I asked Mathew if he had had a nice weekend. To open the discussion, I mentioned that my husband I had taken advantage of the lovely weather in Brighton to play tennis - one of our favorite activities - almost all day Sunday.

Mathew said that he had a nice weekend, too. "I went to the pub with some friends and family, and spent most of Sunday afternoon in the sun." As he described his relaxing weekend, Mathew's behavior told me he had returned to a calm and positive state of mind.

I started the interview by introducing myself, explaining my role in the company, and describing the business. I also reviewed the details about the open position and told Mathew why the position had become available.

As I finished with the introduction, I asked Mathew what had attracted him to the job.
Mathew explained, "I worked for my last employer for ten years. I really want to experience a new company and apply my knowledge in a different organization." He also mentioned that he needed new challenges to stay motivated.

Mathew told me that he had been a Project Manager for the last seven years, and had managed budgets over £5 million and teams of twenty or more people. Despite his accomplishments, Mathew realized that his previous job did not allow for enough experience and exposure. He was interested in the opportunities this new position would provide, including interaction with 3rd parties, and experience researching and designing solutions. –

I liked Mathew's answer. I was also happy to notice that Mathew's face was relaxed, which indicated honesty. However, I was still uncertain that Mathew was right for the job. His lack of experience in hands on solution design was a point of concern.

To determine if this was a valid problem, I asked a follow up question: "During your seven years as a project manager, did you ever have the chance or ask to be part of the design solution on a project you managed?"

Mathew leaned back in his chair, and his face tightened into the expression he had displayed on the elevator. He answered very abruptly, "My job was to be the project manager. I was not asked or compensated to do anything else." This reaction was all I needed to asses this candidate.

I continued the interview, giving Mathew several opportunities to disprove my assessment, but my conclusion remained unchanged. Mathew had the experience to do the job, but he did not have the natural Will to succeed or exceed expectations. We had called for an applicant who *could be an effective influencer across all levels of the organization.* Judging by his lack of motivation in the past, Mathew would not be willing to go above and beyond in the future.

For the Interviewee

This section will discuss how a job applicant should approach an interview. Even if you feel your personal interview skills are sufficient, there is always room for improvement.

For an individual to learn he first needs the will to do so...

There are several factors you should keep in mind and steps you should take every time you prepare for an interview:

Before the Interview

- Make sure you understand the difference between a weak CV (curriculum vitae) and an attention-grabbing CV.

- Research the employer and/or the available position.

- Familiarize yourself with the position requirements and be sure you meet them.

- Prepare relevant stories that illustrate your strengths and demonstrate knowledge

- Determine what the employers are looking for in a prospective employee.

- Polish your communication skills, including **non verbal cues** like facial expressions, eye contact, and other body language.

- Formulating intelligent questions to ask the interviewer.

- Prepare answers to the questions you anticipate from the interviewer.

During the Interview

- Present a professional appearance, including appropriate attire, well-groomed hair, minimal accessories, fragrance, and make-up.

- Speak slowly. Practice voice control, including pitch and tone.

- Be honest, enthusiastic, and assertive.

- Manage questions effectively by providing evidence of positive attitude and competency.

- Answer questions directly and clearly. Be sincere and professional.

- Indicate interest in the field by describing career goals.

After the Interview

- Make notes and evaluate the interview process.

- Evaluate the company and asses your interest in the position.

- Send a thank you note or email to the interviewer (the day of the meeting or soon after).

How to Succeed in an Interview

You've prepared for the interview. Based on your research about the employer, you know you are qualified for the job. You've practiced describing yourself and answering hard questions. You've even done a trial run to make sure you will arrive on time, and tried on the outfit to make sure your appearance is perfect. Now, you're supposed to relax…

Tune Your Frequency and Identify Quadrant Placement

When you arrive, introduce yourself to the interviewer and make sure your nerves are under control. Then, *listen.* Pay attention to the questions so you know exactly what the interviewer is really asking.

Before the interview starts you must identify the interviewer's communication channel and determine where he currently fits in the S&W Quadrant. You can do this by asking your own questions before the formal interview begins. Ask the interviewer about his time with the company, or what his specific position requires of him.

Getting some background information about his work experience and knowledge of the organization will help you to place the individual in the appropriate segment of the quadrant. Then you can communicate on his level.

For example, pretend you are meeting with your interviewer Karl Peters. He receives you at the foyer and walks you to the interview room. Karl may ask about your travel, etc. You politely and briefly respond, "Good, thank you." But then, you take the opportunity to manipulate the conversation to your advantage. Open a new discussion with something like, "This company seems to be a great company to work for. How long have you been working in the organization?"

Karl responds, "Seven years. I moved with the company through a transfer from Germany to the UK three years ago as a Programme Manager for the operations department, and was promoted about six months ago to Director of Operations in the UK.

As Karl speaks, you observe his facial expressions, tone of voice, and body language. Does he reflect enthusiasm? Boredom? Irony? etc.
You notice that when Karl mentioned his promotion, his eyes lit up and his body language projected s a sense of achievement. Karl is proud of himself for being successful in this company.

You now know where Karl currently fits within the quadrant: High Will/ Low Skill. Karl is classified as High Will, because he is obviously proud of his new achievement and probably has plans ways to improve the department.

You might mistakenly assume that Karl is High Skill because he has been promoted. But remember, you have to determine where Karl fits *right now*. He has only been in his current position for six months.

Throughout the interview, you focus on making sure that all of your answers are formulated to accommodate Karl's High Will/Low Skill needs. You use your responses to support his enthusiasm and communicate to him your thoughts and ideas about how can you help to support him and his plans in this new role.

Calibrating your interview answers to the interviewer's position on the quadrant will guarantee a positive and successful interview.

12 – How to Get What You Want

The ultimate purpose of the Quadrant is to get what you want in a given conversation, situation, or relationship. But before learning how to get what you want, you must understand your deeper expectations. *Why* do you want this outcome? What are you going to do with this outcome? How are you going to sustain or keep this outcome?

We all know the story of the magic lamp. There once was very unhappy man who received a dirty old lamp for his birthday. As he wiped the lamp clean - POOF! - out popped a genie!

The genie states, "I shall give you three wishes. You may have anything you like." So the poor man thinks for a minute and says, "I would like a billion dollars." The genie responds, "You shall have it," and grants the wish.

The genie asks, "Anything else?" The man thinks for a while. Then - he decides - "I would like a VW Bug with A/C, power locks, power windows, 10-disc changer - you know, the works." Again the genie consents, "Your wish is my command. What is your last wish?"

"Hmmm." says the man, "I think I'll save my last wish for a rainy day."

"OK, suit yourself," says the genie.

Now happy, the man gets in his new VW and drives quickly off to tell all of his friends about his good fortune. Despite the rain that has begun to fall, the man is giddy. He turns on the radio and starts to sing along with a familiar commercial. "Oh, I wish I was an Oscar Meyer Wiener (sausage)…"

You can imagine what happens next.

What a shock for the man! Sure, we laugh because the story is funny. But the moral is important:

Be careful what you wish for, because you will most likely get it.

By following a structured approach you will be able to focus on the end goal and remembering **why and what** you wanted, without losing focus through the journey.

The Five Steps

1. Define what you want.

Focus on what you want. Picture the end result you desire with as much detail as possible. A clear vision will pull you forward. Don't worry about failure, as that focuses your attention on what you *don't* want.

2. Measure what you want.

Success hinges on your desire and the belief that it's possible. Measure your belief by identifying the doubts that are holding you back. Once you become aware of these weaknesses, they will begin to lose their power.

3. Analyze and commit to your goal.

Consider all of your options. Don't focus on whether or not you will succeed; instead concentrate on the various strategies you can implement. You are worthy of whatever you choose, so embrace the plan with confidence!

4. Implement and take action.

Forget what you think you "should" be doing. Look at the results of your analysis and take action, Listen to your intuition, and allow your instinct to guide your action. Inspired action is satisfying and effective!

5. **Appreciate and manage the results.**
Look for the signs that your desire is beginning to manifest into reality. When you see the first hint - don't stop! Continue with the same actions, propelled by the evidence that success is imminent.

At this point, we are able to use our will to show intention. We have developed a passion for life and our purpose. We simply become what we think we can become. Instead of using ego, use kindness (Dr. Wayne Dyer).

The Karma Effect

Too few people recognize the power of the spoken word or the human mind. Like the self-fulfilling prophecy mentioned earlier, whatever outcome you focus on will come to pass. Unfortunately, we tend to fixate on the negative possibilities; so many outcomes are the opposite of what we really want.

Whatever energy you put out into the universe will return. If you use destructive behavior and language, you will get an equally negative response. The Karma effect is helpful if you're sending out positive energy, but what about situations in which you lose control and allow anger or violence to slip through your barriers? That is why we must learn to control our anger.

Planning for the Outcome: What Do You Do When You Get What You Want?

Did you know winning the lottery can destroy your life? There's not a single person who would expect a gift of millions to be accompanied by great hardship. Yet, research shows that sudden wealth usually leads to broken marriages, troubled children, legal difficulties, and otherwise ruined lives. Few people realize the kind of impact a dramatic financial windfall can have on their lives.

Having tremendous power without *control* can be devastating. In other words, you can have everything you want, but if you don't know how to manage your life, you are doomed to failure.

To avoid a collapse, you must *create* your wish list with a plan in mind, rather than randomly hoping for success.

Baby Steps

Set small objectives that will lead to your ultimate goal. Consider this for a minute: people who wish for a *successful and happy* day usually achieve that goal. If your goal is to become wealthy, wish for each day to be successful. Even if only 85% of your days are a success you will still arrive at your destination. And the chances of achieving success in small increments are much higher than your chances of suddenly winning millions. Is this not a better plan?

Success builds on itself. As you proceed, you will learn the things you must do to achieve your objective. When you finally arrive you will realize that, not only did you have fun on your journey, but you also reached your destination without ruining your life or anyone else's.

You have also developed self esteem, a vital element for continued success, happiness, poise, power, peace, and joy.

Conclusion

The Skill and Will Quadrant was designed to help leaders learn how to best manage and communicate with individuals. The Quadrant is based on the factors of skill and will and is used to weigh an individual's strengths against his or her weaknesses. To be effective at communicating and encouraging production, leaders and communicators must carefully evaluate an individual's level of motivation (will) and training (skill).

In the simple but ever-changing relationship between skill and will, an individual's will is controlled by his or her level of skill. Inversely, person's level of skill is also dictated by his or her level of will. The objective of the Skill and Will Quadrant is to identify specific strategies to improve and maintain a person's level of both skill and will. By making an adjustment to either skill or will, we can produce positive results in ourselves, our employees, and our attempts at communication.

By cross-referencing these traits on the Skill and Will quadrant, leaders and communicators can determine if their employees or participants are capable of handling tasks independently or if they will need motivation to complete specific tasks or comprehend ideas. The manager can then recognize, interpret, and manage each employee or participant based on his or her specific needs. The Skill and Will Quadrant provides specific strategies for communicating with individuals in each quadrant.

- High Will and Low Skill: Guide
- High Will and High Skill: Delegate
- Low Skill and Low Will: Direct
- Low Will and High Skill: Motivate

Pairing opponents within the Skill and Will Quadrant is another effective means for communicating your message. For instance, you can play one person's high skill and low will off of another person's high will and low skill. Two opponent's opposing levels of skill and or/will can actually complement one another and offset or counteract the negative effects of the low skill or will.

Remember, the Skill and Will Quadrant is not designed to help you bend people to your will. This method cannot, and should not, be used to attempt to *change* people. Rather, the Skill and Will Quadrant should be used to prime your audience to *hear your message*.

Furthermore, evaluation and adjustment must occur every time you interact with an individual. Placement in the Skill and Will Quadrant is dynamic, not static. Accurate implementation of Skill and Will communication strategies requires that you be in tune with your audience's specific placement in the Quadrant at any given time.

Summary of Steps

1. Identify where the individual fits in the quadrant using Key Questions.
2. Pay attention to each participant's body language and verbal cues to reaffirm placement in the Skill and Will Quadrant.
3. Identify whether Skill is driving the will or vice versa
4. Recognize, Interpret, and Manage each individual based on his or her specific needs
5. Identify an opposing force for each individual - the opponent.
6. If possible, group the individual with an appropriate opponent(s) for all activities.
7. If an opponent doesn't exist within the group, make sure the individual does not pair up with someone who has matching levels of skill and will. In this situation, you should take on the role of the opponent and partner with the individual.

The goal of this approach to communication is to help you better explain *why* your message is important for all of your listeners, to motivate them to listen, and to help them perceive change as an improvement to their personal situations, rather than an inconvenience.

You simply cannot communicate a complex and complete message to listeners unless you appeal to *each one independently*.

Learning about skill and will is not about the *what*, but the *why*. I hope that you've digested *why* this method is important, *why* this approach works, and *why* I believe so completely in its potential to bring about great change. If you have identified and processed the *whys* of the Skill and Will Quadrant, I have succeeded in my approach and my application.

Glossary of Terms

Blanchard Situational Leadership Model – Developed by Ken Blanchard in the 1960s, this model is the best known example of situational leadership theory. Blanchard's method teaches leaders to evaluate the needs in a particular situation and assume the most appropriate style of leadership. This model fails to address the reality that an individual's placement within the matrix is dynamic, not static.

Conviction – an unshakable belief in something without need for proof or evidence; the power of conviction enables communicators to convince their audience that their message is of importance.

Frequency – every individual has a unique communication style, like a personal radio or channel. This communication style is broadcast through our frequency. Communicators must tune to their audience's frequency in order to best transmit their message.

Key Questions – questions a communicator uses to set the tone for training and identify each participant's placement within the quadrant; also used to break the ice, establish an open and accepting environment, and introduce the purpose of the training.

Neuro Linguistic Programming (NLP) – Developed in the early 1970s by Richard Bandler and John Grinder, NLP is used by psychologists as a tool to influence behavioral change. The goal of NLP is to influence decisions by manipulating emotions, beliefs, and internal representations.

Opponent Quadrant – pairs individuals with opposite levels of skill and will in order to improve both participants' quadrant placement. The Opponent Quadrant relies on the "Opposites Attract Principle" to help communicators develop the most effective training, teaching, or communication strategy possible.

Recognize, Interpret, Manage – the method of identifying, placing, and working with individuals in each area of the Skill and Will Quadrant. Considers the *why* of an individual's placement as opposed to looking only at *where* the individual falls in the matrix.

Skill – an evident and substantial quality which describes our ability to adequately complete a particular task or activity

Skill and Will Quadrant – represents four distinctive skill and will states of being and examines the relationship between different levels of skill and will. The quadrant was designed to help managers and communicators better communicate with people. The Skill and Will Quadrant is an improvement over Blanchard's Situational Leadership Model because the quadrant takes into account the fluid state of skill and will.

Will – our personal level of desire to do or not do a particular task or activity

Index

www.ingramcontent.com/pod-product-compliance
Lightning Source LLC
Chambersburg PA
CBHW050109210326
41519CB00015BA/3893